The Month of the Precious Blood of Our Lord Jesus Christ

**Following Pious Exercises
to Which Indulgences are Attached**

Rev. Fr. Marin de Boylesve, S.J.

Translated and annotated by
E.A. Bucchianeri

The Month of the Precious Blood of Our Lord Jesus Christ

Following Pious Exercises to Which Indulgences are Attached

Rev. Fr. Marin de Boylesve, S.J.

Translated and annotated by
E.A. Bucchianeri

Batalha Publishers
Fátima, Portugal

About this edition: translation from the 2nd French edition published by C. Darveau of Quebec, (1882). This new reprint edition published by Batalha Publishers, Fátima Portugal, © 2022. Edited and annotated by E.A. Bucchianeri, © 2022.

Original Imprimatur given to the French Edition:
✠ Imprimatur apud S. Hyacinthum, 30 (May?), 1882.

✠ Reimprimatur, E.A. Archpus Quebecen, Quebeci die 18 decembris, 1882

TABLE OF CONTENTS

About this Edition ... 10

About the Author Fr. Marin de Boylesve ... 11

Note on the Precious Blood Indulgence ... 25

FIRST NOVENA

The Blood of Jesus Prefigured in the Old Testament

> First Day 27
> Second Day 29
> Third Day 31
> Fourth Day 34
> Fifth Day 36
> Sixth Day 37
> Seventh Day 39
> Eighth Day 40
> Ninth Day 41
> Tenth Day 42

SECOND NOVENA

The Blood of Jesus in the New Testament

Eleventh Day 45
Twelfth Day 46
Thirteenth Day 48
Fourteenth Day 51
Fifteenth Day 55
Sixteenth Day 56
Seventeenth Day 57
Eighteenth Day 59
Nineteenth Day 62
Twentieth Day 64

THIRD NOVENA

The Blood of Jesus in the Church and in the Sacraments

Twenty-First Day 67
Twenty-Second Day 69
Twenty-Third Day 71
Twenty-Fourth Day 72
Twenty-Fifth Day 75
Twenty-Sixth Day 77
Twenty-Seventh Day 78

Twenty-Eighth Day 79
Twenty-Ninth Day 80
Thirtieth Day 81

The CONCLUSION of the MONTH of the PRECIOUS BLOOD

Thirty-First Day 82

Pious Exercises in Honour of the Precious Blood

Offering of the Blood Shed
    from the Right Hand of Christ 84

"Little" Chaplet of the Precious Blood 86

Chaplet of the Precious Blood 93

The Prayer of the Seven Offerings
    to the Precious Blood 102

Three Offerings of the Precious Blood 106

A Jaculatory Prayer 110

An Offering 110

Feast Days of the Most Precious Blood 111

Long Live the Blood of Jesus!
   My Treasure! 112

APPENDIX

Chaplet of the Precious Blood
   in Honour of the Blood Shed
      from the Five Wounds 115

Litany of the Most Precious Blood 120

The Prayer of St. Gertrude 123

Offerings in Reparation
   for the Outrages to the Precious Blood ... 124

Blood of Jesus, Help Me!
      A Prayer for Aid 128

A Prayer for Protection through
   the Power of the Most Precious Blood 129

Prayer to the Precious Blood
   Invoking the Help of Mary 131

The Chaplet of the Holy Wounds 132

Indulgenced Prayers to the Precious Blood

For the Glory of Jesus 143

For the Conversion of Dying Sinners 144

For Reparation and the
      Needs of the Church 145

For the Souls in Purgatory 145

The Anima Christi of St. Ignatius 146

Quotations of St. Gaspar del Bufalo on Devotion to the Precious Blood 147

Illustration Credits 150

About this Edition

About this edition: translation has been taken from the 2nd French edition published by C. Darveau of Quebec, (1882). The translation features British spelling and includes new material not in the original, such as the biography of the author, annotations, illustrations, and the material in the Appendix.

E.A. Bucchianeri

About the Author

Fr. Marin de Boylesve was born on November 28, 1813 at the Château de la Coltrie in the commune of Saint-Lambert de la Potherie near Angers. He came from a distinguished aristocratic family whose name can be traced back many centuries as seen in Abbé Jean-Baptiste Ladvocat's *Dictionnaire historique portatif* (1755). Fr. Marin descended directly from Eslienne Boyliaue (or Boilyeve), the great statesman and the principal adviser of St. Louis IX, King of France. Other illustrious ancestors included intrepid knights, one in particular also named Marin joined the cause of King Henry IV. After the Battle of Arques, the king called him 'his beloved knight', granted him a heredity knighthood in 1597, then was made Seigneur de la Maurouziere in 1598 thereby granting him the right to add three gold fleur-de-lis to the top of his arms and bear the signs of the Order of St. Michel in his escutcheon. He was also appointed lieutenant-general of Anjou and councillor of state as a reward for his dedication. Another Marin Boylesve appears in the family line, the third to hold the name, and was in service to King Louis XIV as manager of his hôtel. Loyal to the French King and to their Catholic faith, many members of the family were forced to emigrate during the French Revolution, but some members stayed behind in their beloved France. Fr. de Boylesve would recall a favourite family story, of how his grandmother was imprisoned in Angers by the Revolutionaries and managed a daring escape on the road during a prisoner transfer to the local castle. While she pretended to pick up a dropped package, a solider kicked her into the ditch. She took the opportunity to flee to a nearby house. However, when they threatened to imprison those harbouring escaped prisoners, she bravely marched straight in to the Revolutionary Office and gave herself up to ensure the safety of those who sheltered her. The revolutionaries did not dare risk upsetting the populace as her father was the former mayor of Angers before the Revolution and loved by the people. They decided to let her return to her father's house.

Fr. de Boylesve was the last direct descendant of his distinguished line, having followed the call to enter the Company of Jesus, or Jesuits, which also is a remarkable story of a predestined vocation. The Jesuits were persecuted due to fears they were growing in power and wealth. Pressured by the royal courts of Europe, Pope Clement XIV suppressed the Society, forcing members of the order to renounce their vows and go into exile. They were expelled from France in 1764. Fr. de Boylesve's mother, Clémentine de Livonnière, made a solemn promise on the day of her wedding that if God permitted the Jesuits to return to France and she was granted a son, she would offer him to the order and entrust him to it. As mentioned, Fr. Marin was born in 1813, a year before 1814 when Pope Pius VII restored the Society. Tragedy struck when Marin's father died, Marin was only ten months old at the time, but keeping her promise his mother dutifully sent him for his education at the age of ten to the Jesuit Fathers of Montmorillon. The moment he arrived at the school and saw a Jesuit for the first time who happened to be the Superior of the college Fr. Michel Le Blanc, he heard an inner voice say to him: "Little one, that is what you will be."

Fr. de Boylesve entered the school as a student and was destined never to leave the Jesuits. In 1831 he turned eighteen, a year after the July Revolution of 1830, which saw the rightful king to the French throne Charles X overthrown. His heir, Henry V the 'Miracle Child', was forced into exile at the age of ten, his throne usurped by the man who had been approached to be his regent, Louis-Philippe, Duke of Orléans. The events of the times burned the hearts of the faithful as the historical church of the royal family, Saint-Germain-l'Auxerrois, was profaned. Paris was sacked, and wayside devotional crosses and shrines over large areas of France were destroyed as Catholic legitimist symbols of Charles X, even those which had no royal significance or connection to the king.

Fr. Marin had just completed his schooling when he formally announced his decision to enter the Society, the historic events of the previous year and their aftermath no doubt influencing his decision. Writing to his grandmother he declared: "The course of my studies completed I could not remain without doing anything. God will ask us for an exact account of all the moments He gives us. Full of this thought I ardently wished to serve my country and the Church especially. At a time when both are in such great peril, as a Frenchman and as a Christian, I felt the need to throw myself into the thick of the fray. To take place in the first rows under the banners of religion whose triumph alone can bring glory and happiness back to my homeland, to serve immediately under my first head Jesus Christ, to be one of His companions, seemed to me the most glorious at the same time as most useful for my neighbour. Immense advantages, treasures of happiness and glory, the hundredfold from this life of all that I would give to the Lord, all of these promised in the gospel by Jesus Christ, strongly attracted me to be generous. What more could I do than give myself? (...)"

His family strongly opposed, especially as he was the last direct heir to the Boylesve house, but his mother let him go despite the great sacrifice, no doubt she understood God was accepting her promise to give him to the Jesuits, and not just for his education but now was asking for his whole life, a bitter dreg for her down to the last drop of the cup.

He entered the Novitiate in 1831 at Estavayer in the canton of Fribourg in Switzerland with two other students. As they arrived at their new school, they rang the doorbell at the moment the house clock struck three. The Father who received them remarked: "You are entering at the hour of the Sacred Heart." This introduction to a new school would once again give Fr. de Boylesve a sign regarding the future work he would one day accomplish, although on this occasion he did not know it at the time. He made his first vows at the Maison du Passage on October 10, 1833. He studied philosophy and then in 1835 became a supervisor at the Collège de Mélan, a position he held for one year. He remained in the same college until 1842 where he was in succession professor of grammar, humanities and rhetoric. He thoroughly enjoyed his work with the students, writing in 1837:

"I find this job a lot of fun, despite the hardships that come with it. I have forty students; I love them and I try to spare nothing to make them good Christians, educated Christians capable of one day rendering true service to religion and to the state. It is the sight of such a noble ending that sustains and animates me." In the same letter he continues, regarding his concern for his family, "(...) what the only important thing is, is everyone behaving well and does he remember the motto of the family, RELIGIO, PATRIA? For me who gave up everything, even my name which will be extinguished in my person, I remember it, and God grant that I am consumed and that I use myself in the service of one and of the other."

Although renouncing his aristocratic life he never gave up its noble spirit represented by the family motto, an ardent loyalty to the Catholic faith of his forefathers and his country. In the title pages of his texts he included the family crest of three crosses and motto: RELIGIO, PATRIE – "Faith and Country". Those who knew him and his 'military' style ways said he was just like the loyal intrepid knights of old.

At the end of 1842 he returned to France. He took theology courses at Laval for four years. Instinctively he was drawn to the writings of St. Thomas Aquinas and steered clear of new systems that deviated from the philosophical teachings of the Seraphic Doctor. In 1846 theology training completed, Fr. Boylesve was sent by his superiors to Angers, then in his third year at Notre-Dame d'Ay. In 1848 he was appointed to Brugelette, where he occupied the chair of philosophy. One student who fondly recalled Fr. de Boylesve and his time at Brugelette said his arrival was providential. His classes were easy to follow his manner clear and crisp, but this is not all that gained the respect of the students. In 1848 they were restless as revolution was in the air, Louis-Philippe I, who had overthrown Catholic King Charles X was now in his own turn overthrown. Rising above and beyond what was required of his philosophy courses, Fr. Boylesve seized the opportunity like a knight-commander of old to direct the lazy students yet bursting with energy towards something constructive: Catholic action to fashion them into vigorous young men of service for Church and country. With his apostolic action he captivated the students with his literature classes, speaking on many subjects from philosophy, history, politics both ancient and modern. He particularly drew them with his catechism lessons on the Council of Trent, his clarity and enthusiasm captivating them.

As Fr. de Boylesve loved his students he was equally admired and loved by them, earning the nickname 'The Captain' as a mark of respect. The students composed a military style tune for his birthday, the refrain remaining popular and hummed everywhere: "Courageous Captain, lead us into battle." A student recalls: "I understood all that was apostolic about his action on us. We can sum it up by saying that he made it his mission to preach to us always and everywhere the contemplation of Saint Ignatius on the Reign of Jesus Christ as it is given in the Exercises." In 1851 Fr. Boylesve was sent to Vannes where he was made prefect of studies, his nickname 'The Captain' following him. In October 1853 he left the post and resumed teaching philosophy, a position that he would keep for a long time, either in Poitiers or in Vaugirard.

Known to be quiet and reserved when on his own, it was another matter when he was teaching or publicly speaking. He was incapable of remaining silent or softening his direct manner of expression when it was a question of truth, and did not hold back when it came to defend the Faith and the Church against unbelievers, becoming as noted like his knight-ancestor of old, charging forth to give chase and defeat any bold rascal on the field of battle albeit with his tongue and writings rather than with a literal sword. His attitude is quaintly summed up by the art critique he once gave of the statue of the fountain of St. Michael in Paris, complaining with slight annoyance that the mighty archangel was made to look too carefree and benevolent when dispatching Satan: "See then, it is that he seems to spare him!" He was also a zealous worker and relished activity. He once wrote: "I challenge my superiors to give me too much work." In addition to his religious duties and teaching, he was a prolific writer, his output seeming to have no end. He wrote on a myriad of subjects and in different genres, from devotional booklets and pamphlets to history, literature, philosophy, Biblical dramas, summaries of the Church Fathers and Doctors, his own sermons, studies of the Scriptures, Our Lady, the Exercises of St. Ignatius just to name a few, there were always more plans for further works in progress, his room filled with notes and notebooks. He was always studying as well, also making it a practise to read through the entire Bible every year. One might call him a workaholic in today's terms, but it was noted he believed in a time and a place for everything and diligently managed his hours. He enjoyed recreation time, especially going for walks, and did not sacrifice rest. Despite his zest for work, he disapproved of a few young professors who sacrificed too much sleep and recreation time for their studies, endangering their health. Yet, while sparing of his time, he was ever charitable and ready to help another all for the glory of God.

In September 1870 Fr. de Boylesve was sent to the College of Le Mans, Notre-Dame de Sainte-Croix, when the Franco-Prussian war was raging and France suffered the indignity of invasion. The humiliation felt by the country also struck the pious and patriotic Fr. de Boylesve to the core: "I searched through the memories of my life; I do not remember ever having felt greater pain than this, not even when I learned of my mother's death. This humiliation of France, the Eldest Daughter of the Church, thus succumbing before Prussia, the Eldest Daughter of Protestantism, in the face of the whole world, is something unheard of."

The Messenger, the magazine of the Apostleship of Prayer run by the Jesuits, began spreading the visions of St. Margaret Mary, declaring the only way France would be saved from her enemies was to embrace the devotion to the Sacred Heart. The message inspired Fr. de Boylesve. He became a chaplain to the Catholic Papal Zouaves forces sent to defend the French Motherland from the Protestant invaders, giving them rousing sermons: "Clotilde, inspiring faith in Clovis, saved the Franks and slaughtered the Germans at their feet ... Joan of Arc by her standard delivered France from the English! Your standard is the Sacred Heart." The Zouaves placed the Sacred Heart on their banner. Fr. de

Boylesve also busily spread Sacred Heart badges of wool for the soldiers to pin on their uniforms, for they were in high demand. A gifted and inspiring preacher, his sermons encouraged them onward, even when they were driven back in defeat by the Prussians to where the soldiers remarked: "This man can lead us to the fire tomorrow; we would gladly be killed for him."

Fr. de Boylesve is fondly remembered today in Catholic circles in France for his work as the director of the Apostleship of Prayer in Le Mans through which he contributed to the spread of devotion to the Sacred Heart. On October 17, 1870 Fr. de Boylesve was appointed to preach at the Visitation of Le Mans upon St. Margaret Mary for his subject, who at the time was a Blessed. He also preached upon another mystic who had died within their own times, Mother Marie de Jesus (1797-1854) from the convent des Oiseaux of Paris who had received revelations from the Sacred Heart that were favourably recognised by the Archbishop of Paris. On June 21, 1823 the Sacred Heart revealed to Sr. Marie that He desired France be consecrated to His Sacred Heart by the King, and that a chapel be built and dedicated to Him, and the feast of the national consecration be formally celebrated every year. "After my sermon," recounts Fr. Boylesve, "the Mother Superior expressed to me her astonishment at my silence with regard to an almost similar order that Our Lord had given to Blessed Margaret Mary on June 17th, 1689. I confessed that in our college, which had barely opened for a month, I had not found the letters of the Blessed One and that I was unaware of the apparition and the order she was telling me about. I promised to make good this omission." Apparently at that time, the Sacred Heart's requests to St. Margaret Mary for a shrine and the national consecration of France by the King were not yet widely known.

True to his word, filled with his characteristic zeal for faith and country, doing what he could to extend the reign of Jesus Christ through his beloved homeland and secure its safety, the very next day he repaired his omission by publishing a pamphlet featuring the prophecies of St. Margaret Mary and Mother Marie de Jesus entitled "Triumph of France by the Sacred Heart", composing a special prayer of consecration to be said, which the Zouaves said every Friday as hope in the Sacred Heart was sorely needed. Paris was threatened with destruction by bombardments, then starvation by the invading Prussians, having commenced a siege around the city in September 1870. The siege continued until January 1871, the citizens reduced to dire circumstances. The zoo animals were slaughtered for food, the populace also living off of stray animals and rats. While the Prussian advance had ceased, humiliation still ensued when France suffered defeat at the hands of the Prussians with the establishment of the German Empire, also losing the territory of the Alsace-Lorraine to the victors. The troubles were not over. From March to May 1871 Paris fell into the clutches of the anticlerical socialist Communards, rebels revolting against the new government of the Third Republic. Blood ran in the streets, historical buildings burned, including the Tuileries Palace. The anticlerical Communards also executed the Archbishop of Paris, Georges Darboy, fulfilling the prophecy of St. Catherine Laboure. This horrific turn of events, combined with the circulation of prophecies foretelling the destruction of Paris was at hand, the faithful no doubt felt doom hung over the city. The times were desperate. After several reprintings, including a full reproduction of the text by Fr. Ramiere in the 'Messenger' newsletter issued by the Apostleship of Prayer, more than 330,000 copies of Fr. de Boylesve's pamphlets of the 'Triumph of the Sacred Heart' were circulated. It contributed to the rapid spread devotion to the Sacred Heart and bolstered the call to have the Universal Church consecrated to the Sacred Heart, also to build a national shrine on Montmartre in atonement for the atrocities committed by the Communards who began their uprising there. Construction began in 1875, the cornerstone was laid on June 16, 1875, the day Bl. Pius IX encouraged all the faithful to pray the consecration to the Sacred Heart using the special formula composed by the Sacred Congregation of Rites for the 200th anniversary of the apparition of the Sacred to St. Margaret Mary. The construction of Sacre Coeur was at last completed in 1914.

As for Fr. de Boylesve, in addition to his

efforts to spread devotion to the Sacred Heart of Jesus, he worked unceasingly at many other endeavours, not only as director of the Apostolate of Prayer in Le Mans, but also with the Confraternities of Saint Joseph such as that of the Good Death, and also the Confraternity of the Agonizing Heart, the Work of Campaigns, Conferences of St. Vincent de Paul, Workers' Circles. He still appeared to dare all and sundry that they would never be able to find enough work for him to do. He amazed all that he was never at a loss for a subject to preach upon. He could easily vary his sermons to where it appeared he never preached the same way twice, and always captured his hearers' attention. One day out of curiosity a hardened sinner walked in to listen to him preach and left a converted man. When Fr. Boylesve wasn't working, he was praying. There was no question that he maintained a deep spiritual life.

He was transferred to Vaugirard in 1875, returning to Le Mans two years later in 1877. Three years later his teaching came to an end at the college there with the decree of March 29, 1880 issued by the French minister for public education prohibiting the Jesuits from engaging in their educational apostolate, only the first of several anticlerical laws that would be passed in France over the next decades. Fr. Boylesve admitted he was on the verge of tears saying his last Mass for the students in the chapel before the school closed. Yet, he remained as active as ever despite this terrible blow, preaching, giving catechisms and continuing his writing, tackling the problems of their day threatening both the Church and society, his work includes this beautiful devotional book to the Precious Blood so closely related to the devotion to the Sacred Heart.

He continued working despite his old age, until the end of 1891 when his activity was curtailed. He was struck with various ailments, first a tormenting dermatitis that remained with him, then inflammation of the blood that restricted his activities for many weeks, although he managed to say Mass and continue his writing, until at last he was struck with paralysis, unable to walk or speak. Clutching his rosary and his crucifix, the ever zealous 'priest-knight' of the Vendée gave up his soul to God in February 22, 1892 and was buried in the Jesuit cemetery of Sainte-Croix.[1]

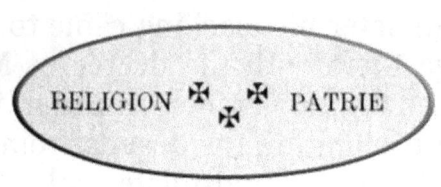

---

[1] Biographical information from 'Necrologie. Le Père Marin de Boyleseve, in 'Lettres de Jersey', Vol.XII, No. 1 (April 1893)

Note on the Precious Blood Indulgence

Pius IX (1850) granted seven years and seven quarantines of indulgences for each day of the month consecrated to the Precious Blood of Our Lord Jesus Christ, in whatever day of the year it is commenced, when it is done in a church or a public oratory. He also granted, under the usual conditions, a plenary indulgence, in the course of the month, or for one of the following seven days, to those who had attended at least ten times the exercises of the Month of the Precious Blood.

He grants three hundred days of indulgences each day to those who make the Month of the Precious Blood in particular, plenary indulgence the last day or one of the seven days that follow.

(Note: The New Advent Catholic Encyclopedia has clearer and slightly different information regarding the indulgences: Indulgences, for the public devotion: seven years and seven quarantines each day; plenary indulgence on any day in July or 1-8 August, after having assisted eight times at a public function under the usual conditions; if the devotion be held privately three hundred days each day with plenary indulgence on 31 July, or 1-8 of August (Pius IX, 4 June, 1850). For this practice any other month or any period of thirty days during the year may be chosen [Raccolta, 178] E.A. Bucc.)

The Blood of the Redeemer,
with Moses and Solomon

FIRST NOVENA

The Blood of Jesus Prefigured in the Old Testament

First Day – *Anima omins carnis in sanquine est.* (Levit. 17:14)   For the life of all flesh is in the blood.

The soul of all flesh is in the blood.[2]

Blood contains all the scattered elements in the animal's body. Scientists call it: 'runny flesh'. It is through the blood that the soul gives life to the body. The blood leaves and returns to the heart. And so under the action of the soul the heart circulates this precious liquid which traverses all the members and all the organs, bringing to each one the elements which they

---

[2]   The Latin scripture says 'anima' which literally would translate as 'soul': 'The soul of all flesh is in the blood.' In English versions of the Bible, 'anima' has been translated as 'life', even in the Douay-Rheims Bible: 'The life of all flesh is in the blood.' Theologically, yes, the soul when still present in the body gives life to the body, the soul departs at death and life is no longer present in the body, therefore it is not incorrect to say 'life' for 'anima' here, note we say something is 'animated' when it has life, is 'lively'', or 'life-like'.   Here, however, Fr. De Boylesve makes a very interesting and deep meditation when concentrating on the literal meaning of the sentence that the '*soul* is in the blood.'.

need to repair themselves.

After having honoured the Sacred Heart of Jesus with a special devotion, we felt the need to extend this devotion to the Precious Blood which leaves It and which constantly returns to take up a new impetus, like the rivers which start from the Ocean never cease to return after having watered the valleys and the plains. - It is especially through the blood that the soul spreads life in the body and that it makes its presence felt there. Let us therefore love to contemplate the most Blessed Soul of Jesus at the centre of His Sacred Heart, as on a throne from which It presides and governs all the organs and members.

O Precious Blood, unite Thy double movement with me, so that all my intentions, starting like Thee from the Heart of Jesus, return there incessantly to be renewed, purified, vivified and deified.

ಖ ♦ ಖ

Second Day – *Faciamus hominem (Hebr. Adam) ad imaginem et Similtudinem nostram.* (Genesis 1:26) "Let us make man to our image and likeness."

The name of our first father (Adam) also means 'man' and 'red', and the word 'dam' means 'blood'. Also the blood is often taken for the whole man. A father says to his son: 'You are my blood.' As we have just recalled, the blood sums up the man. It first sums up the whole body; then it is like the environment which the soul uses to animate the body. Honour therefore the Blood of Jesus; it is the blood of Adam, the blood of man, but a pure and Immaculate Blood, a noble and generous Blood; finally, in Jesus, it is a Divine Blood. And this Blood is our blood. By human nature we are the same blood as Jesus. The blood of Adam, the blood of Noah flows in our veins as in That of Jesus who is truly our Brother.

This is not enough: by the communication of grace, by baptism, and above all by Holy Communion, this Divine Blood exerts on our souls an influence of supernatural life by virtue of which Jesus is not only for us a Brother, but a Father, a second Adam, a second Noah, in the order of grace.

(Creation of Adam)

Christian, recognize your dignity: *Agnosce christiane, dignitatem tuam.*[3] Be worthy of the blood flowing in your veins and live the life of Jesus. *Noblesse oblige:* woe to you, if, son and degenerate brother, you come to dishonour the Blood of Jesus, your Father and your Brother!

☙◆❧

---

[3] Fr. Marin seems to be alluding to a passage in Baruch (4:3) "Ne tradas alteri gloriam tuam, et dignitatem tuam genti alienae.' (Give not thy honour to another, nor thy dignity to a strange nation.) Recognise your dignity and Who you belong to by His Precious Blood. Do not disgrace your noble bloodline through sin!

Third Day – *Vox sanguinis fratis tui clamat ad me de terra.* (Genesis: 4:10) "The voice of thy brother's blood crieth to me from the earth."

These are the words that God addressed to Cain after he murdered Abel. The Voice of the Blood of Jesus, Whom we have crucified, the Voice of this Blood poured out by the hand of the executioners whom our crimes have armed, this Voice cries louder than that of the blood of Abel. It first cries out for mercy; for this Blood was shed for our salvation. But if we trample on the Blood that was to save us, if we are insensible to the Voice of this Blood when It cries out for mercy, on a day like that of Abel, a greater one than that of Abel, It will cry for vengeance. It is a crime to shed innocent blood, the blood of the just; so what can be said of the crime of one who after having shed the Blood of a God, increases ingratitude to It, to despise and profane It? On the Day of Judgement Jesus will show forth His Wounds to us, His Heart half opened by the lance; these were like so many fonts through which flowed the Blood that was shed to atone for our sins and to obtain forgiveness for us. They were to be fonts of mercy, grace and life for us. Indifference will make them sources of anger; and this Blood which was to purify and sanctify us, will become like the fuel of the

Cain and Abel

avenging fire which will burn the sinner during eternity without consuming him.

However, of all the abuses that man can do to the Precious Blood of Jesus, there is none that cries more than that of despair. It is true that if Cain said, "My crime is too great," - I who have shed Blood, not only of a brother, not only of a just one, but of my God and my Saviour, I who after having been covered with this Blood by Baptism, nourished with this Blood by Holy Communion, despised It, profaned It, soiled It by sins, it seems I should cry out in my turn: "Yes , my crime is too great for me to be pardoned." *But this Blood still cries out for mercy, and this Voice is stronger and greater than that of my ingratitude.*

Therefore I can hope, I must hope and I do hope.

Fourth Day – *Lavabit (...) in sanquine uvae pallium sum* (Genesis 49:11)   "He shall wash ... his garment in the blood of the grape."

These words addressed to Judah by the dying Jacob apply to Jesus, Son of Judah. One day Jesus will wash His garment in the blood of the grape. The garment represents the Saviour's Body: His real Body and His Mystical Body. The real Body of Jesus was bathed in His own Blood during the scourging, the crowning with thorns, the crucifixion. The Mystical Body, which is the Church, is daily washed in the Blood of Jesus offered on the altar. This is where the blood of the grape, by the consecration, becomes the Blood of Jesus.

Let us unite our sufferings with those of Jesus and we will be purified in His Blood. Trials have but the end and the effect of making us expiate our frailties and our vanities, of detaching us from pleasures of the senses and worldly honours. From the Heart of Jesus, crushed by sorrow like grapes in the wine press, comes forth pure Blood which is given to us in the Eucharist. This Blood will fill us with a holy intoxication, and forgetting the earth and the flesh, we will be transported above all that is material and of the senses.

"The Mystical Grapes"

Fifth Day – *Et fuit sanguis in tota terra Aegypti* (Exodus 7:21)   "And there was blood in all the land of Egypt."

Moses smites the waters of the river with a rod, and all the waters of Egypt are changed into blood. The rod of Moses recalls the cross of Jesus. By virtue of this cross the peoples represented by the waters are transformed and vivified in the Blood of Jesus. See after the Passion the Apostles, the martyrs, the virgins and the faithful. What boldness! What consistency! What purity! What dedication! What fervour!

The blood was a deadly plague for Egypt, but the Blood of Jesus is for the world the Source of Life.

Are you weak, lukewarm, languid? Go to the Cross, meditate on the Passion of Jesus, contemplate Jesus scourged, crowned with thorns, crucified.   Drink through Holy Communion the Blood and the Water which flowed from the Heart of Jesus. If the mere sight of this Divine Blood shed to save you would be enough to revive your hope and your love, what will the participation in this Precious Blood received in the Holy Eucharist not do?

༂◆༃

Sixth Day - *Erit autem sanguis (vobis) in signum in aedibus, ... et videbo sanguinem, et transibo vos.* (Exodus 12:13) "And the blood shall be (unto you) for a sign in the houses ... and I shall see the blood, and shall pass over you."

The blood (of the immolated lamb) will be a sign (to recognize) your houses and I will see this blood and I will pass (without knocking).

A dreadful night is brewing. The exterminating angel is about to strike dead all the first born of Egypt. The people of Israel were ordered to eat the pascal lamb, figure of the Lamb of God, figure of Jesus immolated on the cross to deliver us from the tyranny of the infernal Pharaoh. God commanded the Hebrews to mark the doors of their houses with the blood of the lamb that they were to sacrifice and eat. 'At the sight of this blood', adds the Lord, 'I will pass without striking you'.

And so, after the sacrifice of the Mass, after Holy Communion, we are marked with the Blood of Jesus. At this sight the exterminating angel withdraws; before this Blood, which is so formidable for him, the devil flees in terror.

ഗ♦ര

Seventh Day – *Sine sanguinis effusion non fit remissio* (Heb. 9:22) "Without shedding of blood there is no remission."

In the greater part of the Law of Moses sacrifices of blood played a central role. Almost always the legal cleansing is done by the blood of victims. This blood was the figure of That of the Holy Victim of Calvary: it is to the shedding of this Divine Blood that we owe the remission of our sins.

Let us join our blood to That of the Saviour. Following the example of the martyrs, like the holy penitents, we shed our blood to accomplish what is lacking in the Passion of Jesus Christ - What then can the Passion lack? - As for the Victim, Whose merit is infinite, nothing is missing. But, if we do not apply the infinite merits of the Divine Blood to ourselves through voluntary penance, our sins will not be erased. So by penance let us seek to immerse ourselves in the Purifying Blood, and, like Naaman coming out of the waters of the Jordan, we will become as pure as a child who has just been born into spiritual life by Baptism.

O Jesus, by Thy Precious Blood, fill me with a holy inebriation which inspires me with contempt for pleasures of the senses and the courage of holy penitence.

Eighth Day - *Sanguis tuus super caput tuum.* (2 Kings 1:16) "Thy blood be upon thy own head."

This was David's judgement against the young Amalekite who boasted of having killed King Saul. What, then, do those deserve who through sin have dealt the King of kings the death blow? But here, by a wonder of mercy, if the Blood of Jesus falls upon the head of the sinner, it is to purify him. This Blood first falls upon the head, seat of intelligence, and gently inclines it under the yoke of faith. And faith engenders hope.

Knowing by faith that Jesus shed for me even the last drop of His Blood, I hope by the virtue of This Blood for the forgiveness of my sins, and for the grace of resisting temptations and repressing my evil inclinations. Hope, in turn, produces charity. On the one hand, the Father, by giving us His only Son, has given us everything with Him; on the other hand, the Son by giving us all of His Blood gives us His own Life. What more could He do for us than die to save us? But also how could I not love the One who shed all His Blood for me, for me a sinner, for me who is the cause of that cruel outpouring?

꧁♦꧂

Ninth Day – *Pulli ejus lambent sanguinem* (Job 39:30) "Her young ones (eaglets) shall suck up blood."[4]

The eagle soars above the highest mountains, and it fixes its gaze on the sun. Let us rise by faith, above the highest thoughts of human reason, and contemplate the Divine Sun hidden under the Eucharistic clouds. Faith will reveal to us the Blood of Jesus there. A drop of blood animates the eagle and excites him to battle. Likewise the Blood of Jesus, like a generous wine, will excite us to battle; It will inspire us with a taste for sacrifice.

Let us contemplate that forehead crowned with thorns and all bloodied, those feet pierced and transformed into fonts of Blood, that Heart half-opened and letting out the little Blood that still remains, the cross, finally, tinted and penetrated with Divine Blood, we approach, apply our lips on this sacred wood and on these bloodied Wounds: the all-spiritual savour of this

---

[4] This is a meditation on the passages of the eagle mentioned in Job, a figure of the Church: (39:27-30) "Will the eagle mount up at thy command, and make her nest in high places? She abideth among the rocks, and dwelleth among cragged flints, and stony hills, where there is no access. From thence she looketh for the prey, and her eyes behold afar off. Her young ones shall suck up blood: and wheresoever the carcass shall be, she is immediately there."

Precious Blood will fill us will disgust for sensual sweets, and will fill us with a very divine ardour for suffering and for humiliation.

֍

Tenth Day – *Et apersus est sanguis eorum super vestimenta mea.* (Isaiah 63:3) "And their blood is sprinkled upon my garments."

In the eyes of the Prophet, the Saviour appears as a warrior returning from combat. The Prophet asks who this noble and proud fighter is. - "I am," replied the hero, "I am the One who preaches justice and who fights to save." - Why, continues Isaiah, why is thy garment red like that of the winegrower when he comes out of the press? - "I am the only One that can tread the press," replies the Saviour, "and I crush My enemies under My feet in My fury, and their blood has spurted onto My garments." - In reality, however, Jesus was only covered with His own Blood. But as He had taken upon Himself your sins and as, in the daring expression of St. Paul, He who did not know sin, He who was innocence itself, He had made himself sin, by taking full responsibility: *Eum qui non novertaa peccatum pro nobis peccatum fecit.* (2 Cor.

5:21),[5] therefore His completely Immaculate Blood represents the blood of sinners for which It is substituted, and it is permissible to say that it is sin that covered Jesus with blood, and that it is to crush sin that Jesus Himself was crushed in His Passion.

And we in the struggle against sin, against temptation, have we resisted to the point of blood? *Nondum enim usque as sanguinem restitistis, adversus peccatum repugnantes.* (Heb. 12: 4) "For you have not yet resisted unto blood, striving against sin."

꽁●꽃

---

[5] The full verse from St. Paul reads: "Him, who knew no sin, he hath made sin for us, that we might be made the justice of God in him." The Douay-Rheims Bible explains that "he made sin for us" indicates Christ took on our sins and became a sin-offering for them as a victim for our sins.

SECOND NOVENA

The Blood of Jesus in the New Testament

Eleventh Day – *Hostiam et oblationem noluisti corpus autem aptasti mihi.* (Heb. 10:5)
"Sacrifice and oblation thou wouldest not (of the old law): but a body thou hast fitted to me."

It was impossible for the blood of goats and bulls to wash away sins. Also, entering the world by the Incarnation, the Saviour said to His Father: "You have not accepted as a host and as an offering the flesh and blood of animals: but of the purest blood of the Virgin Mary You have formed Me a Body and in this Body flows a Blood which, by virtue of the hypostatic union, is Divine Blood; and I have said 'I Am here, I have come.' For it is written about Me that I will do Your will, O God." So from the very first moment of the Incarnation, Jesus ceaselessly saw His own Blood shed for our sins. We can say that the Passion from that point on was started in the Soul of Jesus, and on the other hand, in His Heart.

If we knew in advance the sorrows that await us, it would be impossible for us to taste the slightest sweetness in this life. Also, even when we foresee an inevitable suffering, such is our horror of all that is unpleasant to us that we try to conceal, to soften, to forget, to delude ourselves about this future which threatens us.

But Jesus knew and saw from His entry into this world all the trials that awaited Him; He did not try to look away, to hide the gravity of it. So this was His life for thirty-three years, or rather, a continuous death!

We are the authors of this long agony, of this continual Passion. Let us at least be sympathetic, and accept with resignation the evils which befall us and which we have so well deserved.

ஐ♦ஓ

<u>Twelfth Day</u> - *Et postquam consummati sunt dies octo, ut circumcideretur puer, vocatum est nomen ejus Jesus.* (Luke 2:21) "And after eight days were accomplished, that the child should be circumcised, his name was called Jesus."

The great Name of Jesus is the price of blood. This Name means Saviour, to be the Saviour, Jesus must shed His Blood. The drops of Blood from the Circumcision are only the initial payments of the waves which must one day flow from the cross. Let us adore the first fruits of this Divine Blood, and let us unite our compassion with that of Mary and of Joseph.

"The Circumcision"

Let us look deep into the Heart of the Divine Infant, there we will see there the joy He feels at beginning to suffer for our salvation.

Suffering terrifies us, the cross terrifies us! Let us start with small 'sugar stack' sacrifices.[6] Let us accept with resignation the little crosses of each day; let us free ourselves little by little, today from one thing, tomorrow from another: and we will become capable of carrying with Jesus the great and heavy cross of Calvary.

Thirteenth Day – *Et factus est sudor ejus sicut guttae sanguinis decurrentis in terram.* (Luke 22:44) "And his sweat became as drops of blood, trickling down upon the ground."

The sight of the Passion alone was enough to seize the Heart of Jesus and to make on It a deadly impression; but what breaks It with sorrow is the thought that so many cruel

---

[6] There seems to be a charming word-play in the original French text: Fr. De Boylesve has 'sucrifices' here – meaning 'sugar stacks', but the word 'sacrifices' is implied. We can daily add the little sacrifices until they pile like a sugar loaf, and, we can taste the joy or 'sweetness' of offering the sacrifices little by little, until we can bear the heavier crosses thereby learning how to feel the *joy* in sacrificing.

sufferings will be useless for those millions of souls who will obstinately reject grace. In the presence of this ingratitude, this Heart of the Saviour, so delicate and so generous, beats with unspeakable violence, and the repressed Blood escapes through all the pores: it is from this that sweat of Blood reduces Jesus to agony.

And at the sight of this sweat with which our sins have flooded the members of our Saviour, we remain cold, insensitive, indifferent!

Already, while Jesus was watching, praying, sweating Blood and seeing Himself reduced to agony, the Apostles, even the chosen apostles Peter, James and John, instead of watching and praying, had fallen asleep a few steps away from their Master.

So it still is today at the sight of the Blood of Jesus still flowing on our altars, uselessly for so many obstinate souls to their loss, while we in turn sleep in a blithely tranquil manner.

However, it was above all the indifference of His most faithful friends, those who by profession and by commitment should have shown themselves the most faithful, it was above all this spiritual sleep of those who are called the good ones, which provokes the sweat of Blood of the Saviour.

So when will we finally wake up from our drowsiness?

༄◆༅

Fourteenth Day – *Peccavi tradens sanguinem justum.* (Matt.27:4) "I have sinned in betraying innocent blood."

These are the words of Judas to the princes of the priests, when seeing Jesus condemned, he repented of having delivered Him up and came to bring back the money he had received as a price for his betrayal. We see it; nothing is omitted to repair the crime: restitution of money, confession of sin. It is not the courage which Judas lacks: it was necessary to expose himself to all the fury of the enemies of Jesus by a reparation which was to confuse their malice and their iniquity! However Judas was still lost! What was lacking in his penance?

He did not understand the virtue of the Blood he had just delivered; he did not hear the Voice of this Blood which still cried only for mercy. After having thrown the price of his treason at the feet of the iniquitous judges, after such a daring, such a generous, such a compromising outburst, *why did he not come and throw himself at the feet of Jesus!* This is where he needed to cry out: *Pecavi traden sanguinem justum.* I have sinned, betraying the blood of the innocent.

Judas Returning the Silver

Jesus would not have left him time to finish, but, like the father of the prodigal son, He would have admitted the repentant traitor to a new kiss, to the kiss of reconciliation which would have forever effaced that of his betrayal. What consolation would this return not have brought to the Heart of Jesus, in the anguishes and sorrows of the Passion!

Too often, alas! The opportunity is offered to us to provide the Heart of Jesus with consolation of this kind! Too often we betray It through our faults. So, instead of abandoning ourselves to discouragement and despair, let us come back to Jesus, let us throw ourselves at His feet, let the Blood that escapes from His Heart flow on our hearts, and with His friendship, with His grace, He will restore to us confidence, innocence and peace.

ಖ ♦ ಛ

Pilate Washing His Hands

Fifteenth Day – *Innocens ego sum a sanguine justi ejus.* (Matt. 27:24) "I am innocent of the blood of this just man."

No, Pilate, no, you are not innocent of the Blood of this Just Man; you could defend Him and you should have. You should have: you recognized His innocence and His justice; you recognized the jealousy, the malice, the iniquity of the accusers. Ignorance cannot therefore excuse you. - You had power at hand; one signal from you, and your soldiers would have appeared, the crowd stirred up by the pontiffs would have suddenly dispersed with their leaders. You cannot allege weakness. - So you could have defended the Just One and have saved Him. By saving Him you would have saved yourself; by losing Him, by delivering Him, you are lost!

But if there was no excuse for Pilate, if Pilate was not innocent of the Blood of this Just Man, what excuse can be imagined for a Christian, who through sin, still sheds the Blood of Jesus?

What excuse can I make for myself? Ignorance? But I know what Pilate did not know, I know that Jesus is God, I know that by sinning I trample on the Blood of a God. I know and I believe that it is for me, to save me that Jesus shed His Blood. Pilate did not know that Jesus was the Saviour. He could have known it, Jesus was quite ready to teach it to him, and if after asking: What is the truth? *Quid est veritas*? He would have waited for the answer, he would have learned Who this Just One, this Innocent was; but finally if Pilate is guilty for having feared to learn and know more than he wanted about the person of Jesus, I who know it, I who believe that Jesus is my God and my Saviour, what excuse then can I bring when, by sin, I despise a Blood that I know to be the Blood of a God shed to save me?

ಬಿ♦ಜ

Sixteenth Day – *Sanguis ejus super nos et super filios nostros.* (Matt. 27:25) "His blood be upon us and our children."

Yes, O my Divine Jesus, Thy Blood falls upon us; but this vow in our mouth has a very different meaning from that which was on the lips of the Jews. We are more guilty than them, it is true, since we have more lights and we know what they ignored, knowing that Thou art the King of glory, the Saviour, the Messiah, God Incarnate, we deserve that Thy Blood falls back upon us like the avenging waters of the Deluge on the heads of the corrupt men, like the rain of fire on Sodom; we hope, however, that this Innocent Blood will only fall upon us to purify and sanctify us.

O Blood Divine, be for us a rain of mercy and of grace, and not a rain of fury and vengeance; be for us a rain of fire, but of a fire which consumes only our iniquities and which sets our hearts ablaze with the flames of Divine charity.

༄༅༈

<u>Seventeenth Day</u> – *Apprehendit Pilatus Jesum et flagellavit.* (John 19:1) "Pilate took Jesus, and scourged Him."

The Blood of Jesus spurted from the blows that were unleashed upon His virginal flesh. By this torture, as humiliating as it is cruel, the Saviour wants to expiate those guilty pleasures and delights that dishonour bodies and souls.
Will we continue to spare our criminal flesh? Will we finally understand the obligation and the necessity of the mortification of the senses, either to repair the mistakes made, or to prevent new falls?

The executioners rise up to strike. Their arms grow weary, without exhausting the patience of the August Victim. The blows no longer fall on flesh, but on bones that can already be counted: *Dinumeraverunt omnia ossa mea.* (Psalm 21:18) ("They have numbered all my bones.") The Sacred Body of Jesus, from head to toe, is nothing but one huge wound.

And we, after an attempt at penance, we are soon tired, and it is not long before we relapse into our habitual sluggishness. When, then, will we be resolved to exhaust ourselves for the One Who exhausted Himself for us? When, then, to save ourselves, will we have the courage to suffer with Jesus, Who to save us did not shrink from any suffering?

಄♦ఇ

Eighteenth Day - *Et plectentes coronam de spinis posuerunt super caput ejus.* (Matt. 27:29) "And platting a crown of thorns, they put it upon his head."

His Head had escaped the blows of the scourging; it is necessary that a particular torture be invented by the cruelty of the executioners to

make flow from this sacred Head the Blood of the Saviour. Behold your King with the crown that his subjects have braided for Him. Count and measure those hard and long thorns which penetrate to the bones and which descend just to the eyes. The slightest pain which affects the head produces intolerable discomfort throughout the body, from this experience judge the sufferings of Jesus after the crowning of thorns. - What will it be like then when He will have to carry the cross? This rough wood, while walking, will continually strike the crown and drive the thorns more and more into the Head of the August Patient One - But on the cross, what torture! If the Head of the Saviour does not touch the wood, It falls towards the chest and by Its weight enlarges the Wounds of the hands and feet. If Jesus tries to hold His Head upright, the wood of the cross pushes back the thorns and makes them penetrate further. Also under these cruel thorns, the Blood does not stop flowing, It floods the eyes, It goes down to the lips, it wets the whole face.

Let us collect the drops of this Precious Blood to atone and to efface those many criminal thoughts that we have so often entertained.

Nineteenth Day – *Postquam venerunt in locum qui vocatur Calvariae ibi crucifixerunt eum.* (Luke 23:33) "And when they were come to the place which is called Calvary, they crucified Him there."

They crucified Him. The word is short, but the operation is slow and cruel. Consider, one after the other the nails which pass through the feet and hands of the Divine Crucified One; hear the hammer blows driving in the nails. See the Blood spurting from these four fonts, *Videbunt in quem transfixerunt.* ("They shall look on him whom they pierced." John 19:37) These hands which have spread only blessings, these feet which have traversed Judea bringing the One Who passed only to do good: *Pertransiit benefaciendo,* ("Who went about doing good." Acts 10:38) here they are now immobilized and reduced to the inability to act.

This then is how men reward the services they have received. Try to do good, they will band together to prevent you from walking and acting. Let us work, however, go wherever the service of God and neighbour calls us, but instead of concordance and recognition, let us expect from most men nothing but obstacles, opposition and ingratitude.

೫♦ಡ

Twentieth Day – *Unus militum lanceo latus ejus aperuit et continuo exivit sanguis et aqua.* (John 19:34) "But one of the soldiers with a spear opened his side, and immediately there came out blood and water."

The Blood represents the Eucharist, the Water represents Baptism. Baptism and the Eucharist: one, the first Sacrament, the other, the most great, recall all the sacraments and the Church itself, which is born by Baptism and which is sustained by the Eucharist. Therefore let us go to the Heart of Jesus. There is our cradle; there we are born into the Christian life. We are His Blood. Let us live for Him and through Him. This Sacred Heart is the font source, we are the streams; He is the sun, we are the rays. Separated from the source the stream dries up, separated from the sun the ray is extinguished. Separated from the Heart of Jesus, our life, our virtue, vanishes and disappears. United with His Sacred Heart like the stream at the source, like the ray from the sun, our Christian life and our supernatural virtue are preserved and will not cease to grow.

Let us remain at the foot of the cross, let us contemplate Jesus crucified; we find all the sacraments represented and realized in His Person.

THIRD NOVENA

The Blood of Jesus in the Church and in the Sacraments

Twenty-First Day – *Baptismo qua ego baptizor, baptizabimini.* (Mark 10:39) "And with the baptism wherewith I am baptised, you shall be baptised."

The mother of James and John asks Jesus for her two sons the first two places. Jesus addresses this question to the two brothers; "Can you drink of the chalice that I drink of: or be baptised with the baptism wherewith I am baptised?" It was about the Passion which was to be both a chalice and a baptism. Now the Passion is the measure of glory. Without hesitation, James and John respond: "We can." But they do not insist here on baptism.[7] Behold

---

[7] Fr. De Boylesve seem to be pointing out they were desirous of the glory their mother wanted for them in having the prime places next to Jesus, they were no doubt thinking of a kingly chalice of honour, not knowing what Christ truly meant. Hence, they were 'not insisting on the baptism' they must undergo. One must suffer with Christ to be His follower, hence, everyone must suffer in one form or another the baptism of the Passion, which we first enter into through the sacrament of baptism.

Jesus covered with sweat of Blood, scourged, crowned with thorns, crucified, and as a result of this triple punishment, all inundated with His own Blood; here is His baptism. Now, it is not only James and John who must participate in this bloody and terrible baptism, St. Paul extends this obligation to all Christians. Every Christian is baptised in the Blood of Jesus, baptised in Jesus Christ, baptised in the death of Jesus Christ, buried with Jesus Christ by baptism to die in sin. (Cf. Rom. 6: 3, etc.) The baptism in Jesus Christ is the condition of our resurrection to life. *Concepulti ei in baptismo in quo et resurrexistis.* ("Buried with Him in baptism, in Whom also you are risen again," Col. 2:12) By baptism we have put on Jesus Christ: *Quicumque enim in Christo baptizatiestis, Christum induistis.* ("For as many of you as have been baptised in Christ, have put on Christ." Gal. 3:27)[8]. To put on Jesus Christ, it seems to me, to take the form of Jesus Christ, is to become similar to Jesus Christ, and this likeness saves us by making us agreeable to the

---

[8] Of interest, the phrase here is '*induistis*' in the Latin, 'put on' is similar to 'investiture', as to put on a garment, i.e. vestments, etc. To 'put on' Christ is to be clothed in a new garment so to speak where Christ Himself is the garment. Consider the parables Christ told of the wedding garments at the wedding feast, and those clothed with new white garments before the Lamb in the Apocalypse, those garments have been made white by the Blood of the Lamb. Fr. de Boylesve's French text also implies this: "Par baptism nous avons comme revêtu Jesus Christ" ~ "By baptism we have clothed Jesus Christ (on ourselves)."

heavenly Father Who is pleased to see in us as many brothers of His Divine Son; *Quos et vos nunc similis formae salvos facit baptisma.* ("Whereunto baptism being of the like form, now saveth you also". 1 Peter 3:21) But for the resemblance to be perfect, we must mix our blood with the Blood of Jesus, the blood of our tears, the blood of our penance, the blood of our contrition, the blood of continual mortification by accepting the cross of each day.

ஐ♦ଔ

<u>Twenty-Second Day</u> – *Qui autem confirmat nos vobiscum in Christo, et qui unxit nos Deus, qui et signavit nos et dedit pignus Spiritus in cordibus nostris.* (2 Cor. 1:21-22)

"Now he that confirmeth us with you in Christ, and that hath anointed us, is God: Who also hath sealed us, and given the pledge of the Spirit in our hearts."

The Passion was for Jesus Confirmation and anointing. There He was sacred in his Own Blood. [9] The blow which the bishop gives is a memory of the cruel blow which Jesus received from the hand of a valet and of the repeated blows heaped upon Him by the insolence of the

---

9 'Sacred', as in 'sacring', the ancient term for the consecration and coronation ritual of a monarch.

people of the high priest and of the praetorian soldiers. The anointing which the bishop makes on the Christian whom he confirm recalls the Blood, which flowing under the thorns of the crown inundated the Saviour's forehead on the day of His sacring and His coronation. Finally, steadfast firmness, which is the proper effect of the sacrament of Confirmation, is like a participation in the invincible firmness of Jesus, when on the day of His Passion He withstood blows and insults with a face harder than stone and with a diamond forehead. (Isaiah 50: 7, Ezechiel 3: 9)[10]

O Precious Blood, strengthen me, inebriate me, make it so that above all fears I may despise the contempt of the world as well as its fury.

༄༅༅

---

10   "The Lord God is my helper, therefore am I not confounded: therefore have I set my face as a most hard rock, and I know that I shall not be confounded." (Isaiah), and "I have made thy face like an adamant and like flint: fear them not, neither be thou dismayed at their presence: for they are a provoking house." (Ezechiel).   Adamant = a symbolic stone of impenetrable hardness. Historically, the word was applied to actual stones and other substances believed to be impenetrable; in the 17th century the word was used as a synonym for diamond.

Twenty-Third Day - *Hic est enim sanguis meus Novi Testamenti, qui pro multis effundetur in remissionem peccatorum.* (Matt. 26: 28) "For this is My blood of the New Testament, which shall be shed for many unto remission of sins."

Through the Old Testament, God was united with a special people, with the people of

Israel; through the New He unites Himself with all peoples, all those He calls to be part of the Church, the Mystical Body of which Jesus is the Head. The sign of the Old Testament was the Ark of the Covenant, the sign of the New is the very Blood of Jesus: *Hic est enim sanguis mesu Novi Testamenti.*

This Blood is the Blood of the sacrifice visibly shed on the cross for the remission of sins, shed invisibly and mystically on the altar to continue the outpouring of Calvary. It is through this Precious Blood that the Eucharist is the continuation of the sacrifice of the cross.

Let us unite the sacrifice of our blood, of our lives, of our penances, to the sacrifice of Jesus on the altar; through this union we will be confirmed the New Covenant which reunites each one of us to God.

ଊ♦ଓ

Twenty-Fourth Day – *Amen dico vobis, qui jam non bibam de hoc genimine vitis, usque in diem illum cum, cum illud bibam novum in regno Dei.* (Mark 14:25)

"Amen I say to you, that I will drink no more of the fruit of the vine, until that day when I shall drink it new in the kingdom of God."

The Blood of Jesus in the Eucharist is not only the Blood of sacrifice, it is also a beverage: *Sanguis meus, vere est potus.* ("My Blood, is drink indeed." John 6:56) As such It is, under the appearance of wine, this Sacrament, the sensible and effective sign of supernatural life and vigour. Ordinary wine intoxicates with an intoxication that takes away the use of reason and freedom, which submits the soul to the body, which weighs down the body itself, paralyses it and sometimes renders it incapable of movement. The Precious Blood of Jesus received in the Eucharist produces an entirely opposite intoxication, an intoxication which lifts the soul above itself, above the senses, above the whole world. This pure and holy inebriation inspires contempt for pleasures and pain, riches and poverty, honours and humiliation. Lost in God, the soul inebriated with the Adorable Blood of Jesus sees only God, desires only God; it finds Him everywhere; but mainly on the cross and in tribulation: Calvary is its Tabor; it is there that the soul sets up her tent and cries out: *Bonum est nos hic esse.* ("It is good for us to be here." Matt. 17:4) 'Either suffer or die,' she cries with St. Theresa. *Aut pati, aut mori.* - 'No,' it soon continues with St. Magdalene de Pazzi, 'no, not to die, but to still live to suffer': *Non mori, sed pati.*

༄●༅

Twenty-Fifth Day - *Habemus redemptionem par sanguinem ejus.* (Colos. I.14) "In whom we have redemption through His Blood."

It is up to us to unite the blood of our tears and the contrition of our hearts: because without our participation, the Redemption will not be applied to us. Without the Blood of Jesus, the reconciliation of the sinner with God is impossible, but if our blood does not unite with the Blood of Jesus by contrition, there is neither forgiveness nor peace for us. If to redeem us Jesus shed His Blood, it is only just that we shed a few tears over our unhappy state. It is not necessary that these tears be visible, but without spiritual tears, without sincere repentance, one cannot say of the sinner that he has renounced sin, that he has separated from it; one cannot say that he does not want to offend God. How could God return His grace and His friendship to the one who refuses it and who persists in not loving Him? Without contrition, therefore, redemption cannot extend and be applied to the sinner; the Blood of Jesus has flowed for him, but It has not yet flowed *on* him.

If we want to be delivered from our sins, let us weep over them and detest them.

༄♦༅

Twenty-Sixth Day – *Beati qui lavant stolas suas in sanguine Agni.* (Apoc. 22.14) "Blessed are they that wash their robes in the Blood of the Lamb."

Blessed are they who purify their consciences in that Precious Blood by Confession and by absolution. Only then the Divine Blood has the virtue to erase sin and restore life. Only then will we have *a right to the tree of life.* ("That they may have a right to the tree of life "Apoc.) Only then will we have the right to taste the Fruit of Life, suspended from the tree of the cross of which the Sacrifice of the altar is the continuation. This Fruit of Life is Jesus Himself, and we receive It by Holy Communion. Then also, and only then, will we be permitted to enter the Holy City. Becoming again, by absolution, living members of the Church Militant, we will see the gates of the Church Triumphant open for us: *Beati qui lavant stolas in sanguine Agni, et sic potest corum in ligno vitae et per portas intrent in civitatem.* "Blessed are they that wash their robes in the Blood of the Lamb: that they may have a right to the Tree of Life, and may enter in by the gates into the city." (Apoc. 22:14)

༄♦༅

Twenty-Seventh Day – *Justificati in sanguine ipsius, salvi crimus ab ira per ipsum.* (Rom. 5:9) "Justified by His Blood, shall we be saved from wrath through Him."

Only the Blood of Jesus gives our offerings of atonement the virtue of repairing and atoning for sin. The offence being infinite due to the Infinity of the Offended One, it took the infinite virtue of Divine Blood to satisfy Infinite Justice and to appeal for mercy. By ourselves, in vain we will multiply our penances. All that we can do and suffer is finite: a finite good cannot repair an infinite evil.

However, Jesus will not make satisfaction alone. As we have said over and over again, with the Blood of Jesus we must unite our own acts of atonement. Following the example of the Apostle, we must bear upon us the mortification of Jesus Christ.

To the involuntary sufferings which arise without our having sought them, let us add voluntary penances; then, justified in the Blood of Jesus, we will be preserved by Him from the Divine Wrath.

Twenty-Eighth Day - *Tinget sacerdos digitum in sanguine hostiae pro peccato, tangene cornua altaris holocausti.* (Lev. 4:25)

"The priest shall dip his finger in the blood of the victim for sin, touching therewith the horns of the altar of holocaust."

So when we are about to die, the priest will dip his finger in the holy oil, symbol of the Blood of Jesus, and he will touch the various organs of our senses to purify them. So Jesus Himself; dying on the cross, received in His own Blood the last and supreme unction. Blood flowed from His thorn-crowned forehead, to His eyes, to His ears, to His nostrils, to His lips. His chest and loins were covered with the Blood from the flogging. His feet and hands, pierced by nails, were bathed in blood.

What agony! Our passing, however painful it may be, will not come close to that. But, however sad and so cruel, the Blood of Jesus represented by the holy oils will be for us an anointing which will soften the supreme test, at the same time it will strengthen us for the decisive struggle and will transform us into invincible athletes.[11]

---

[11] Obviously a reference to St. Paul applying to the Christian life the example of running a gruelling race or marathon: those that persevere gain the prize of eternal salvation.

Twenty-Ninth Day – Hoc facite in meam commemorationem. (Luke 22:19) "Do this for a commemoration of me."

Do this, do what I just did. Right then, Jesus had just consecrated the bread and the wine and changed them into His Body and His Blood. By His words He conferred on His Apostles the power to consecrate them also and to change the bread and the wine into His Body and into His Blood; He gave them power over His Body and over His Blood, the power to sacrifice Him by the sword of a double consecration.

To this power had to correspond a power no less astonishing, a power which extended over the Mystical Body of Jesus, over the Church, over the members of the Church, the power to grant by absolution supernatural life to the sinner, the power to remit sins by virtue of this Blood that was poured out on the altar.

The priest is therefore the giver of the Blood of Jesus. At the altar he offers It to the Eternal Father for our salvation; at the tribunal of the Sacrament of Penance he pours It spiritually on the guilty soul to restore it to life; at the altar he gives It in Holy Communion to the faithful purified by the Sacrament of Penance.

And we, by our ingratitude, by our insensitivity, by our indifference, we neglect this Precious Blood which for us would be the source of life. However, the priest, by his presence alone, constantly recalls the intimate union that Saviour wanted to establish between Him and us, by instituting the sacraments of Holy Orders, of the Eucharist, and of Penance. *Hoc facite in meam commemorationem.* - "Do this for a commemoration of Me."

༄༅༅

Thirtieth Day – *Et continuo exivit sanguis et aqua.* (John 19:34) "And immediately there came out Blood and Water."

A soldier pierced the side of Jesus while dead on the cross, and through this Wound immediately gushed Blood and Water, symbol of the two main sacraments, of Baptism and the Eucharist, and thereby the Church which is made up above all by these two sacraments. The origin and this formation of the Church coming out from the side of Jesus, recalls the mother of the human race, drawn from the side of Adam by a Divine operation.

Then God introduced the first woman to the first man, and at this sight, Adam was inspired and cried out: "This now is bone of my bones, and flesh of my flesh." And so he proclaimed the unity and the sanctity of Marriage.

That august Sacrament is the symbol of the all-spiritual union of Jesus Christ with the Church that issued from His Heart and of His Blood. It is also the symbol of the intimate union that Baptism and Holy Communion established between Jesus and each one of the faithful.

Let us go to the Heart of Jesus, or rather return. This is the font of our spiritual life; it is from there that the vivifying Blood flows into our souls.

༄༅༅

THE CONCLUSION OF THE MONTH OF THE PRECIOUS BLOOD

Thirty-first Day – *Tres sunt qui testimonium dant in terra: Spiritus et aqua, et sanguis: et hi tres unum sunt.* (1 John 5:8)

"And there are three that give testimony on earth: the spirit, and the water, and the blood: and these three are one."

The Holy Spirit by the outpouring of His gifts attests to the Divinity of Jesus Christ; the water of Baptism by the infusion of grace bears the same testimony; the Blood of Jesus, by the redemption of the world, confirms the two preceding attestations: thus these three testimonies together make but one.

Let us follow the lights and inspirations of the Holy Spirit, then our life as well as our words will be a continual manifestation of the Divinity of Jesus.

Let us live the Christian life received at baptism; then our faith, our hope, our charity will attest to the Divinity of Him Who communicates to such weak men a completely supernatural life.

Let us act under the impulse of the Heart of Jesus; then the Divine Blood circulating in us in an ineffable way will animate us with such vigour and ardour that we will be able to cry out with the apostle: "And I live, now not I; but Christ liveth in me," (Gal. 2:20). Then our actions will be a living testimony of the Divinity of Him Who, by His Blood, has purified, vivified, and sanctified us, and after having lived in time in the life of Jesus by grace, we will live in eternity in the life of Jesus by glory. So be it. Amen.

Pious Exercises in Honour of the Precious Blood

Offering of the Blood Shed from the Right Hand of Christ

(Indulgence of 100 days each time - Plenary indulgence once a month if recited daily for a month, under the usual conditions of Confession, Communion and prayers for the Holy Father.)

Eternal Father, we offer Thee the Precious Blood of Jesus shed for us with so much love and so much pain, from the Wound in His right hand; and by the merits and virtue of this same Blood, we beseech Thy Divine Majesty to grant us a holy blessing, so that by It we may be delivered from our enemies and delivered from all evils. Let us therefore say: *Benedictio Dei omnipotentis, Patris and Filii, et Spiritus Sancti descendat supernos, and maneat semper.* (May the blessing of Almighty God, the Father and the Son, and the Holy Spirit descend upon us and remain forever.) Amen.

Say a *Pater* (Our Father), *Ave* (Hail Mary) and *Gloria* (Glory Be) in honour of the Holy Trinity, in thanksgiving for all blessings received.

"Little" Chaplet of the Precious Blood

(Indulgence of seven years and seven quarantaines once a day. Plenary indulgences once a month if recited daily, under the usual conditions.)

Latin: V. Deus in adjutorium meam intende.
R. Domine, ad adjuvandum me festina.
   V. Gloria Patri, etc.
R. Sic erat, etc.

Translation. V. Come to my aid, O Lord,
R. O Lord, make haste to help me.
   V. Glory Be, etc.
R. As it was in the beginning, etc.

1st Mystery

Jesus sheds His Blood in the Circumcision

Five Our Fathers, one Glory Be.

Prayer: V. Te ergo quaesumus, famulis tuis subveni,
R. quos pretioso sanguine redeministi.

(V. Therefore, we pray Thee, Lord, help Thy servants,
R. Whom Thou hast redeemed with Thy Precious Blood.)

2nd Mystery

Jesus sheds His Blood while praying in the Garden of Olives.

Let us ask for the spirit of prayer.

Five Our Fathers, one Glory Be.
The prayer, *Te ergo,* etc.

3rd Mystery

Jesus sheds His Blood at the Scourging.

Let us ask for the grace of mortification.

Five Our Fathers, one Glory Be.
The prayer, *Te ergo,* etc.

4th Mystery

**Jesus sheds His Blood
during the Crowning with Thorns.**

Let us ask for the grace to despise worldly honours.

Five Our Fathers, one Glory Be. The prayer, *Te ergo,* etc.

5th Mystery

**Jesus sheds His Blood
while Bearing the Cross.**

~

Let us ask for the grace of patience.

Five Our Fathers, one Glory Be.
The prayer, *Te ergo,* etc.

6th Mystery

**Jesus sheds His Blood
during the Crucifixion**

Let us ask for the grace of perfect contrition.

Five Our Fathers, one Glory Be. The prayer, *Te ergo*, etc.

7th Mystery

Jesus shed His Blood and the Water at the Stroke of the Lance.

Let us ask for the grace of final perseverance.

Five Our Fathers, one Glory Be.
The prayer, *Te ergo,* etc.

Concluding Prayer of the Little Chaplet:

Prayer to the Precious Blood

(300 days indulgence each time.)

O Most Precious Blood of Eternal Life, the ransom and redemption of the whole universe, the drink and bath of our souls, Thou Who art ever pleading our cause of men before the throne of God's sovereign mercy; I adore Thee most profoundly, and desire, as far as it is in my power, to compensate Thee for the insults and affronts which Thou art continually receiving at the hands of men, especially of those who rashly dare to blaspheme thee.

And who is there that will not bless this Blood of infinite value? Who is there that will not feel himself inflamed with love for Jesus Who shed it? What should I be if I had not been redeemed by this Divine Blood? What was it that drew Thee forth from the veins of my Lord, even to the last drop? Ah! it was nought else but love.

O boundless love, that has given us this Balsam of salvation! O Balsam beyond price, streaming forth from the well-spring of a boundless love, grant, oh, grant that every heart and tongue may praise, and magnify, and bless Thee, now and for ever, even unto the day of eternity! Amen.

V. Redemisti nos, Dominé, in sanguine tuo.
R. Et fecisti nos, Seo nostro regnum.

Oremus: Omnipoents sempiterne Deus, qui Unigentium Filium tuum mundi Redemptorm constituisti, ac ejus sanguine placari voluisti: concede nobis, quaesumus, salutis nostrae pretium ita venerari, atque à praesenti vitae malis ejus virtute, defendi in terris, at fructu perpetua laetemur in coelis. Qui tecum vivit et regnat in unitate, etc. Amen.

Translation:

V. Thou hast redeemed us, O Lord, in Thy Blood.
R. And thou hast made us a kingdom unto our God

<u>Let us pray:</u> Almighty and eternal God, Thou hast appointed Thine only-begotten Son the Redeemer of the world and willed to be appeased by His Blood. Grant, we beg of Thee, that we may worthily adore this price of our salvation and through Its power be safeguarded from the evils of the present life so that we may rejoice in its fruits forever in heaven. Through the same Christ our Lord. Amen.

ഌ♦ଓ

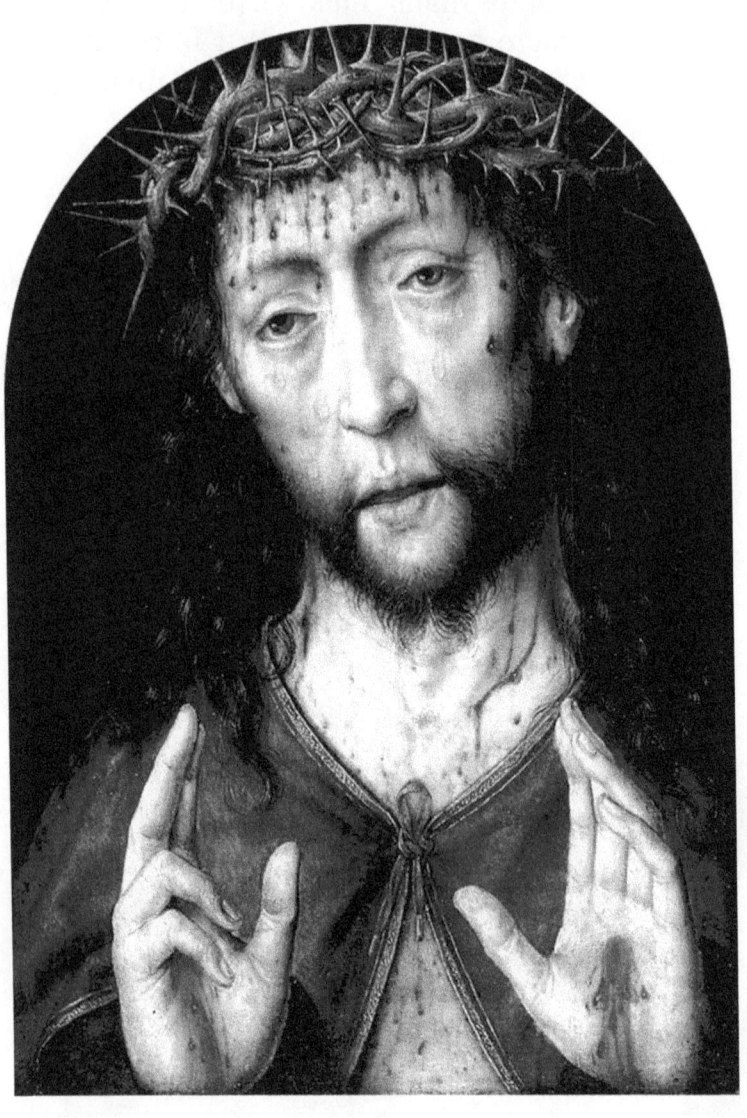

Chaplet to the Precious Blood of Jesus

(Same mysteries as the 'Little' Chaplet, but with the longer official prayers and meditations.)[12]

---

[12] Information regarding the origin of this chaplet: Pope Pius VII., in order to inflame the hearts of the faithful with devotion to the Precious Blood of Jesus Christ, wherewith we were redeemed, granted by two Rescripts, one of May 31, 1809, kept in the acts of the Congregation of Rites, the other of Oct. 18, 1815, in the Archivium of the Archconfraternity of the Precious Blood, erected at St. Nicholas in Carcer, here in Rome –

i. An indulgence of seven years and seven quarantines, once a day, to all who shall say with devotion the Chaplet in honour of the Precious Blood of Jesus Christ.
ii. A plenary indulgence, once a month, to all who, having said it every day for a month, shall Confess and Communicate, and pray for the holy Church, &c.
iii. Three hundred days indulgence, daily, to all who say the prayer, "Most Precious Blood, & c.,".

This Chaplet is composed of seven Mysteries, in which we meditate upon the seven times in which Jesus Christ for love of us shed blood from His most innocent Body; at each Mystery, except the last, we are to say five *Pater noster's* and one *Gloria Patri*; and at the last, three *Pater noster's* only and one *Gloria Patri*; thus making up the number of thirty-three *Pater noster's* in remembrance of the thirty-three years during which the Precious Blood of Jesus flowed in His veins, before it was all poured out for our salvation. The Chaplet ends with the devout prayer, "Most Precious Blood, & c."

(Indulgence of seven years and seven quarantaines each day. Plenary indulgence once a month if said daily, under the usual conditions.)

V. Deus, in adjutorium meum intende.
R. Domine, ad adjusandum me festina.
   V. Gloria Patri, etc.
R. Sicut erat, etc.

Translation: V. Come to my aid, O Lord,
R. O Lord, make haste to help me.
   V. Glory Be, etc.
R. As it was in the beginning, etc.

First Mystery

The first time our loving Saviour shed His Precious Blood for its was on the eighth day after His birth, when He was circumcised in order to accomplish the law of Moses. While, then, we reflect that Jesus did this to satisfy the justice of God for our dissolute lives, let us excite ourselves to true sorrow for them, and promise, with the help of his all-powerful grace, to be henceforth truly chaste in body and in soul.

Five Pater Nosters, (Our Fathers) one Gloria Patri, (Glory Be).

Prayer: V. Te ergo quaesumus, famulis tuis subveni,
R. quos pretioso sanguine redeministi.

**(V. Therefore, we pray Thee, Lord, help Thy servants,
R. Whom Thou hast redeemed with Thy Precious Blood.)**

Second Mystery

Next, in the Garden of Olives, Jesus shed His Blood for us in such quantity that it bathed the earth around. This took place at the sight of the ingratitude with which men would meet His love. O, let us, then, repent sincerely because we have hitherto corresponded so ill with the innumerable benefits of our God, and resolve to make good use of His graces and holy inspirations.

Five Pater noster's *and one* Gloria Patri.

Te ergo quaesumus, &c.

Third Mystery

Next, in His cruel scourging, Jesus shed His Blood, when His flesh was so torn that rivers of Blood flowed from His body in every part, all of which He offered all the time to His Eternal Father in payment of our impatience and our delicacy. How is it, then, we do not curb our anger and our self-love? Henceforth we will indeed try our very best to bear our troubles well, and, despising ourselves, to take peacefully the injuries which men may do us.

Five Pater noster's *and one* Gloria Patri.

Te ergo quaesumus, &c.

Fourth Mystery

Again, from the sacred Head of Jesus Blood poured down when it was crowned with thorns, in punishment of our pride and evil thoughts. Shall we, then, continue to nurture haughtiness, foster foul imaginations, and feed the wayward will in our minds? Henceforth let there be ever before our eyes our utter nothingness, our misery, and our weakness; and with generous hearts let its resist all the wicked suggestions of the devil.

Five Pater noster's *and one* Gloria Patri.

Te ergo quaesumus, &c.

<u>Fifth Mystery</u>

But O! how much of His Precious Blood did our loving Lord pour forth from His veins when laden with the heavy wood of the cross. He made His mournful way to Calvary, so that the streets and ways of Jerusalem, through which He passed, were watered with it! This was done in satisfaction for the scandals and the bad examples by which His own creatures had led others astray on the way to ruin. Who can tell how many of us are of this unhappy number? Who knows how many he himself alone has by his own bad example brought down to hell? And have we done anything to remedy this evil? Let us henceforth at least endeavour all we can to save souls by word and by example, making ourselves a pattern to all of good and holy life.

Five Pater noster's *and one* Gloria Patri.

Te ergo quaesumus, &c.

Sixth Mystery

Still more copiously the Redeemer of mankind shed Blood in His barbarous Crucifixion; when His veins being rent and arteries burst, there gushed forth in a torrent, from His hands and His feet, that saving balm of life eternal, to pay for all the crimes and enormities of the universe. Who ever after this would continue in sin, and so renew the cruel crucifixion of the Son of God? Let us weep bitterly for our bad deeds, and let us detest them at the feet of the sacred minister of God; let us amend our evil ways, and henceforth begin a truly Christian life, with the thought ever in our hearts of all the Blood which our eternal salvation cost the Saviour of men.

Five Pater noster's *and one* Gloria Patri.

Te ergo quaesumus, &c.

Seventh Mystery

Last of all, after His death, when His sacred Side was opened by the lance and His loving Heart was wounded, Jesus shed Blood, and with the Blood there came forth water, to show us how the Blood was all poured out to the last drop for our salvation. O the infinite goodness of our Redeemer! Who will not love Thee, my Saviour? What heart will not consume itself away for love of Thee, who hast done all this for our redemption? The tongue wants words to praise Thee: let us, then, invite all creatures upon earth, all angels and all saints in Paradise, and, most of all, our dear Mother Mary, to bless, to praise, and to celebrate Thy most Precious Blood. Glory to the Blood of Jesus! Glory to the Blood of Jesus now and ever throughout all ages. Amen.

At this last Mystery three Pater Noster's *and one* Gloria Patri *are to be said, to make up the number of thirty-three.*

Te ergo quaesumus, &c.

Then say the following:

O Most Precious Blood of Eternal Life, the ransom and redemption of the whole universe, the drink and bath of our souls, thou Who art ever pleading our cause of men before the throne of God's sovereign mercy; I adore Thee most profoundly, and desire, as far as it is in my power, to compensate Thee for the insults and affronts which thou art continually receiving at the hands of men, especially of those who rashly dare to blaspheme Thee.

And who is there that will not bless this Blood of infinite value? Who is there that will not feel himself inflamed with love for Jesus Who shed it? What should I be if I had not been redeemed by this Divine Blood? What was it that drew Thee forth from the veins of my Lord, even to the last drop? Ah! it was nought else but love.

O boundless love, that has given us this Balsam of salvation! O Balsam beyond price, streaming forth from the well-spring of a boundless love, grant, oh, grant that every heart and tongue may praise, and magnify, and bless thee, now and for ever, even unto the day of eternity! Amen.

VI. Redemisti nos, Dominé, in sanguine tuo.
R. Et fecisti nos, Seo nostro regnum.

Oremus: Omnipoents sempiterne Deus, qui Unigentium Filium tuum mundi Redemptorm constituisti, ac ejus sanguine placari voluisti: concede nobis, quaesumus, salutis nostrae pretium ita venerari, atque à praesenti vitae malis ejus virtute, defendi in terris, at fructu perpetua laetemur in coelis. Qui tecum vivit et regnat in unitate, etc. Amen.

Translation:

V. Thou hast redeemed us, O Lord, in Thy Blood.

R. And thou hast made us a kingdom unto our God.

Let us pray: Almighty and eternal God, Thou hast appointed Thine only-begotten Son the Redeemer of the world and willed to be appeased by His Blood. Grant, we beg of Thee, that we may worthily adore this price of our salvation and through Its power be safeguarded from the evils of the present life so that we may rejoice in its fruits forever in heaven. Through the same Christ our Lord. Amen.

༄●༅

(End of the Chaplet)

The Prayer of the Seven Offerings of the Precious Blood

(Indulgence of three hundred days each time it is said. Plenary indulgence once a month, if recited daily, under the usual conditions.)

Eternal Father, I offer Thee the merits of the Most Precious Blood of Jesus, Thy Beloved Son and my Divine Redeemer, for the propagation and exaltation of my dear Mother the Holy Church, for the safety and prosperity of her visible Head, the Holy Roman Pontiff, for the cardinals, bishops, and pastors of souls, and for all the ministers of the sanctuary. (Glory Be...etc.)

Blessed and praised for evermore be Jesus Who hath saved us by His Precious Blood! Eternal Father, I offer Thee the merits of the Most Precious Blood of Jesus, Thy Beloved Son and my Divine Redeemer, for the peace and concord of nations, for the conversion of the enemies of our holy Faith, and for the happiness of all Christian people. (Glory Be.) Amen.

Blessed and praised for evermore be Jesus Who hath saved us by His Precious Blood! Eternal Father, I offer Thee the merits of the Most Precious Blood of Jesus, Thy Beloved Son and my Divine Redeemer, for the repentance of unbelievers, the extirpation of all heresies, and the conversion of sinners. (Glory Be.)

Blessed and praised for evermore be Jesus Who hath saved us by His Precious Blood! Eternal Father, we offer Thee the merits of the Most Precious Blood of Jesus, Thy Beloved Son and my Divine Redeemer, for all my relations, friends and enemies, for the poor, the sick, and those in tribulation, and for all those for whom Thou willest I should pray, or knowest that I ought to pray.   (Glory be.)

Blessed and praised for evermore be Jesus Who hath saved us by His Precious Blood! Eternal Father, I offer Thee the merits of the Most Precious Blood of Jesus, Thy Beloved Son and my Redeemer, for all those who shall this day pass to another life, that Thou mayest preserve them from the pains of Hell and admit them the more readily to the possession of Thy glory.   (Glory Be.)

Blessed and praised for evermore be Jesus Who hath saved us by His Precious Blood! Eternal Father, I offer Thee the merits of the Most Precious Blood of Jesus, Thy Beloved Son and my Divine Redeemer, for all those who are lovers of the Treasure of His Blood, and for all those who join with me in adoring and honouring It, and for all those who try to spread devotion to it. (Glory Be.)

Blessed and praised for evermore be Jesus Who hath saved us by His Precious Blood! Eternal Father, I offer Thee the merits of the Most Precious Blood of Jesus, Thy Beloved Son and my Divine Redeemer, for all my wants, spiritual and temporal, for the Holy Souls in Purgatory, and particularly for those most forgotten, the souls of priests, and for those who in their lifetime were most devoted to this Price of our Redemption, and to the Sorrows and pains of our dear Mother, Most Holy Mary. (Glory Be.)

Blessed and praised for evermore be Jesus Who hath saved us by His Precious Blood!

℘♦℘

Three Offerings of the Precious Blood

In Thanksgiving for the Privilege of Mary's Immaculate Conception – this was traditionally said before making the Stations of the Cross.

(Indulgence of three hundred days each time it is said. Plenary Indulgence once a month after daily recitation, under the usual conditions.)

Eternal Father, in union with the Most Holy and Immaculate Virgin, and in her name, and in union with all the Blessed in Heaven and all the Elect upon earth, I offer Thee the Most Precious Blood of Jesus Christ in thanksgiving for the gifts and privileges conferred on Thy most obedient Daughter, especially in her Immaculate Conception. I offer Thee also this Most Precious Blood for the conversion of all sinners, for the propagation and exaltation of our Holy Faith, for the conservation and prosperity of the Sovereign Pontiff of Rome and according to his intentions.

Glory be to the Father, etc.

Eternal and Incarnate Word, in union with the Most Holy and Immaculate Virgin, and in her name, and in union with all the Saints and Angels in Heaven and all the Elect upon earth, I

offer Thee Thy Most Precious Blood, in thanksgiving for the gifts and privileges conferred on Thy most loving Mother, especially in her Immaculate Conception. I offer Thee also Thy Most Precious Blood for the conversion of all sinners, for the propagation and exaltation of our Holy Faith, for the conservation and prosperity of the Sovereign Pontiff of Rome and according to his intentions.

Glory be to the Father, etc.

Holy and Eternal Spirit, in union with and in honour of the Immaculate Virgin Mary and in her name, and in union with all the Angels and Saints in Heaven and all the Elect upon earth, I offer Thee the Most Precious Blood of Jesus Christ in thanksgiving for the gifts and privileges conferred on Thy most faithful Spouse, especially in her Immaculate Conception. I offer Thee also this Most Precious Blood for the conversion of all sinners, for the propagation and exaltation of our Holy Faith, for the conservation and prosperity of the Sovereign Pontiff of Rome and according to his intentions.

Glory be to the Father, etc.

Eternal Father, I offer Thee the Most Precious Blood of Jesus Christ in expiation of my sins and for the wants of Holy Church.

Conclude with the following prayer:

Prayer to the Most Blessed Virgin

Mary, Mother of God, most holy and Immaculate Virgin, by the love thou dost ever bear to God, by the gratitude thou hast towards Him for the manifold graces and favours with which thou wast enriched by Him, particularly for the privilege of Immaculate Conception granted to thee alone, and by the infinite merits of Jesus Christ, thy Divine Son our Lord, we pray thee most earnestly to obtain for us a most perfect and constant devotion towards thyself, and a full trust that through thy most mighty intercession we shall receive all the graces which we ask. Certain henceforth of obtaining them from thy great goodness, with hearts overflowing with joy and thankfulness, we venerate thee, and say the salutation which the holy archangel Gabriel made to thee.

Ave Maria, ... (Hail Mary ...), etc.

(End of the Three Offerings)

A Jaculatory Prayer

(Indulgence of one hundred days each time.)

Eternal Father, I offer Thee the Precious Blood in atonement for my sins and for the needs of Holy Church. Amen.

☙♦❧

An Offering

(Indulgence of one hundred days each time.)

Eternal Father, we offer Thee the Blood, the Passion, and the death of Jesus Christ, the sorrows of Mary most holy, and of St. Joseph, in satisfaction for our sins, in aid of the holy souls in purgatory, for the needs of holy Mother Church, and for the conversion of sinners. Amen.

☙♦❧

Feast Days of the Most Precious Blood

The first Sunday of July and the Friday after the fourth Sunday in Lent.

(Note: Fr. De Boylesve simply adds "Plenary Indulgence" under this heading, but doesn't clarify how to gain it here, and so I have listed again the requirements to gain a plenary indulgence for July and August in honour of the Feast of the Precious Blood. E.A. Bucc.)

Indulgences, for the public devotion: seven years and seven quarantines each day; plenary indulgence on any day in July, or 1-8 August, after having assisted eight times at a public function under the usual conditions; if the devotion be held privately three hundred days each day with plenary indulgence on 31 July, or 1-8 of August (Pius IX, 4 June, 1850).

Long Live the Blood of Jesus! My Treasure

(Hymn in honour of the Precious Blood)

There is a good that I desire
A treasure from Heaven that comes to us,
It is He Who I celebrate with my lyre,
It is He for Whom I search at the altar.
And this good alone is what I claim,
This treasure that charms my heart,
The object for which thirsts my soul,
It is the Blood of my Redeemer.

I choose It for my share.
I only live on His love,
And to forever love Him more,
Every day this is what I dream of.
Yes, the good alone I claim,
My sole treasure, my sole happiness,
The object for which thirsts my soul,
It is the Blood of my Redeemer.

Sing His praises day and night,
To adore Him, that is my destiny;
Why should I envy the angels,
Do I not also have their task divine?
It is not here below for the soul,
Happiness, there is no other source.
Yes, the sole good that I claim,
It is the Blood of my Redeemer.

When the thorn of sacrifice
Comes to wound my failing heart
It is a heavenly Chalice
Offering its intoxicating charm.
So what to my soul does it matter
Whether it have sorrows or joys?
All the happiness that I claim,
It is the Blood my Redeemer.

I drink it at every dawn
Without ever quenching my thirst
And in the evening I am caught again,
When close to the altar I sigh ....
And in this desire that inflames me,
I discover my sweetest bliss,
O Jesus, within my soul make grow,
The thirst for Thy Redeeming Blood.

Veneration of the Holy Wounds

APPENDIX

ಙ♦ಙಙ♦ಙಙ♦ಙ

The Chaplet of the Precious Blood

In honour of the Blood shed from the Five Wounds during the Crucifixion.

This chaplet has its own particular set of chaplet beads.

Begin with the **Apostles' Creed**. Then say the following invocation:

May the Precious Blood that flows out from the Sacred head of Our Lord Jesus Christ cover us now and forever. Amen.

THE FIRST MYSTERY

The Nailing of the Right Hand of Our Lord Jesus.

PRAYER: By the Precious Wound in Thy Right Hand and through the pain of the nail which pierced Thy Right Hand, may the Precious

Blood that pours out from there, convert many souls and save sinners of the whole world. Amen.

Our Father (once), Hail Mary (once)---both on white bead. On the twelve beads, say:

Precious Blood of Jesus Christ.
Save us and the whole world.

Glory be, etc.

THE SECOND MYSTERY

The Nailing of the Left Hand of Our Lord Jesus.

PRAYER: By the Precious Wound in Thy Left Hand and through the pain of the nail which pierced Thy Left Hand, may the Precious Blood that pours out from there relieve Souls in Purgatory and protect the dying against the attacks of evil spirits. Amen.

Our Father (once), Hail Mary (once)-both on white bead. On the twelve beads, say:

Precious Blood of Jesus Christ.
Save us and the whole world.

Glory be, etc.

THE THIRD MYSTERY

The Nailing of the Right Foot of Our Lord Jesus.

PRAYER: By the Precious Wound in Thy Right Foot and through the pain of the nail which pierced Thy Right Foot, may the Precious Blood that pours out from there cover the foundation of the Catholic Church against the plans of the evil spirit and evil men. Amen.

Our Father (once), Hail Mary (once)---both on white bead. On the twelve beads, say:

Precious Blood of Jesus Christ.
  Save us and the whole world.

Glory be, etc.

THE FOURTH MYSTERY

The Nailing of the Left Foot of Our Lord Jesus.

PRAYER: By the Precious Wound in Thy Left Foot, and through the pain of the nail which pierced Thy Left Foot, may the Precious Blood that pours out from there protect us from the plans and the attacks of evil spirits and their minions. Amen.

Our Father (once), Hail Mary (once)---both on white bead. On the twelve beads, say:

Precious Blood of Jesus Christ.
Save us and the whole world.

> *Glory be*, etc.

THE FIFTH MYSTERY

The Piercing of the Sacred Side of Our Lord Jesus.

PRAYER: By the Precious Wound in Thy Sacred Side and through the pain of the lance which pierced Thy Sacred Side, may the Precious Blood and Water that pours out from there cure the sick, bring repentance to the dying, and bring us to eternal happiness with God. Amen.

Our Father (once), Hail Mary (once)---both on white bead. On the twelve beads, say:

Precious Blood of Jesus Christ.

Save us and the whole world.

Glory be, etc.

<u>*Conclude with*</u>*:*

Hail, holy Queen, Mother of mercy; our life, our sweetness, and our hope. To thee do we cry, poor banished children of Eve; to thee do we send up our sighs, mourning and weeping in this vale of tears. Turn then most gracious advocate, thine eyes of mercy towards us; and after this our exile, show unto us the Blessed Fruit of thy womb, Jesus. O clement, O loving, O sweet Virgin Mary. Pray for us, Oh holy Mother of God; That we may be made worthy of the promises of Christ.

<u>*Let us pray*</u>*:*

O Most Precious Blood of Jesus Christ, we honour, worship and adore Thee Heal the wounds our souls and wash away the sins of the whole world. O Precious Blood, have mercy. Amen.

Most Sacred Heart of Jesus, Have mercy on us.
Immaculate Heart of Mary, Pray for us.
St. Joseph, Pray for us.
Ss. Peter and Paul, Pray for us.

St. John at the foot of the Cross, Pray for us.
St. Mary Magdalene, Pray for us.
All ye Saints and Angels, Pray for us.

(End of the Chaplet)

෨♦ඏ

Litany of the Most Precious Blood

Lord, *have mercy on us*.
Christ, *have mercy on us*.
Lord, *have mercy on us*.
Christ, hear us.
Christ, *graciously hear us*.
God, the Father of Heaven, *have mercy on us*.
God the Son, Redeemer of the world,
 have mercy on us.
God, the Holy Ghost, *have mercy on us*.
Holy Trinity, One God, *have mercy on us*.
Blood of Christ, only-begotten Son of the Eternal Father, *save us*.
Blood of Christ, Incarnate Word of God, *save us*.
Blood of Christ, of the New and Eternal Testament, *save us*.
Blood of Christ, falling upon the earth in the Agony, *save us*.
Blood of Christ, shed profusely in the Scourging, *save us*.

Blood of Christ, flowing forth in the Crowning with Thorns, *save us.*
Blood of Christ, poured out on the Cross, *save us.*
Blood of Christ, price of our salvation, *save us.*
Blood of Christ, without which there is no forgiveness, *save us.*
Blood of Christ, Eucharistic drink and refreshment of souls, *save us.*
Blood of Christ, stream of mercy, *save us.*
Blood of Christ, victor over demons, *save us.*
Blood of Christ, courage of Martyrs, *save us.*
Blood of Christ, strength of Confessors, *save us.*
Blood of Christ, bringing forth Virgins, *save us.*
Blood of Christ, help of those in peril, *save us.*
Blood of Christ, relief of the burdened, *save us.*
Blood of Christ, solace in sorrow, *save us.*
Blood of Christ, hope of the penitent, *save us.*
Blood of Christ, consolation of the dying, *save us.*
Blood of Christ, peace and tenderness of hearts, *save us.*
Blood of Christ, pledge of eternal life, *save us.*
Blood of Christ, freeing souls from purgatory, *save us.*
Blood of Christ, most worthy of all glory and honour, *save us.*
Lamb of God, Who takest away the sins of the world, *spare us, O Lord!*
Lamb of God, Who takest away the sins of the world, *graciously hear us, O Lord!*
Lamb of God, Who takest away the sins of the world, *have mercy on us.*

V. Thou hast redeemed us, O Lord, in Thy Blood.
R. And made us, for our God, a kingdom.

Let us pray: Almighty and everlasting God, Who didst appoint Thine only-begotten Son the Redeemer of the world, and hast willed to be appeased by His Blood; grant unto us, we beseech Thee, so to venerate (with solemn worship) the price of our redemption, and by its power be so defended against the evils of this life, that we may enjoy the fruit thereof for evermore in Heaven. Through the same Our Lord Jesus Christ, Thy Son, Who liveth and reigneth with Thee in the unity of the Holy Ghost, God, world without end. R. Amen.

The Prayer of St. Gertrude

(An efficacious prayer for the souls in Purgatory and for sinners.)

Eternal Father, I offer Thee the Most Precious Blood of Thy Divine Son, Jesus, in union with the masses said throughout the world today, for all the Holy Souls in Purgatory, for sinners everywhere, for sinners in the universal church, those in my own home and within my family. Amen.

(NOTE: it is said this prayer releases 1,000 souls from Purgatory each time it is said, but under the pontificate of Pope Leo XIII this was declared not to be the case as Our Lord only showed St. Gertrude a vast number of souls entering heaven from purgatory as a result of her faithful and frequent recitation of this prayer. The prayer indeed helps the Holy Souls, but there is no indication Our Lord gave a specific number of souls.)

Offerings in Reparation for the Outrages to the Precious Blood

I

Eternal Father! I offer Thee the merits of the Precious Blood of Jesus, Thy well-beloved Son, my Saviour and my God, for the propagation and exaltation of my dear Mother Thy holy Church, for the safety and prosperity of her visible head, our chief pastor the Bishop of Rome; for the cardinals, bishops, and pastors of souls, and for all the ministers of the sanctuary.

Gloria Patri ...

Blessed and praised for evermore be Jesus, Who hath saved us with His Blood.

II

Eternal Father! I offer Thee the merits of the Precious Blood of Jesus, Thy well-beloved Son, my Saviour and my God, for the peace and concord of Catholic kings and princes, for the humiliation of the enemies of our Holy Faith, and for the welfare of all Christian people.

Gloria Patri ...

*Blessed and praised for evermore be Jesus,
Who hath saved us with His Blood.*

III

Eternal Father! I offer Thee the merits of the Precious Blood of Jesus, Thy well-beloved Son, my Saviour and my God, for the repentance of unbelievers, the uprooting of heresy, and the conversion of sinners.

Gloria Patri ...

*Blessed and praised for evermore be Jesus,
Who hath saved us with His Blood.*

IV

Eternal Father! I offer Thee the merits of the Precious Blood of Jesus, Thy well-beloved Son, my Saviour and my God, for all my relations, friends, and enemies; for the poor, the sick, and the afflicted, and for all those for whom Thou my God knowest that I ought to pray, or wouldst have me pray.

Gloria Patri ...

*Blessed and praised for evermore be Jesus,
Who hath saved us with His Blood.*

V

Eternal Father! I offer Thee the merits of the Precious Blood of Jesus, Thy well-beloved Son, my Saviour and my God, for all who this day are passing to the other life; that Thou wouldst save them from the pains of Hell, and admit them quickly to the possession of Thy glory.

Gloria Patri ...

*Blessed and praised for evermore be Jesus,
Who hath saved us with His Blood.*

VI

Eternal Father! I offer Thee the merits of the Precious Blood of Jesus, Thy well-beloved Son, my Saviour and my God, for all those who love this great treasure, for those who join with me in adoring it and honouring it, and for those who strive to spread devotion to it.

Gloria Patri ...

*Blessed and praised for evermore be Jesus,
Who hath saved us with His Blood.*

VII

Eternal Father! I offer Thee the merits of the Precious Blood of Jesus, Thy well-beloved Son, my Saviour and my God, for all my wants, spiritual and temporal, in suffrage for the holy souls in purgatory, and chiefly for these who were most devout to this Blood, the price of our redemption, and to the sorrows and pains of our dear Mother, most holy Mary.

Gloria Patri ...

*Blessed and praised for evermore be Jesus,
Who hath saved us with His Blood.*

Glory be to the Blood of Jesus, now and forever, and throughout all ages. Amen.

ଃ♦ଽ

Blood of Jesus, Help Me
A Prayer for Aid

In every need let me come to Thee
    with humble trust saying:
        Blood of Jesus, help me!
In all my doubts, perplexities, and temptations,
    Blood of Jesus, help me!
In hours of loneliness, weariness and trials,
    Blood of Jesus, help me!
In the failure of my plans and hopes; in
    disappointments, troubles and sorrows,
        Blood of Jesus, help me!
When my heart is cast down by failure, at seeing
    no good come from my efforts,
        Blood of Jesus, help me!
When others fail me, and Thy grace alone
    can assist me,
        Blood of Jesus, help me!
When I throw myself on Thy tender love as my
    Father and Saviour,
        Blood of Jesus, help me!
When I feel impatient, and my cross irritates me,
    Blood of Jesus, help me!
When I am ill, and my head and hands
    cannot work and I am lonely,
        Blood of Jesus, help me!
Always, always in spite of weakness, falls and
    shortcomings, of every kind,
        Blood of Jesus, help me
            and never forsake me.   Amen.

A Prayer for Protection through the Power of the Most Precious Blood

Lord Jesus, in Thy Name and with the power of Thy Precious Blood, we seal all persons, acts or events through which the devil wants to harm us.

With the power of Thy Blood, Jesus, we seal all destructive powers in the air, on the earth, in water, in fire, under the earth, in the satanic forces in nature, in the abyss of hell, and in the world in which we live today.

With the power of the Blood of Jesus, we put an end to all the interference and actions of the evil one. We beg Thee, Jesus, to send the Blessed Virgin, accompanied by St. Michael, St. Gabriel and St. Raphael, and all the choirs of angels to our homes and work places.

With the power of the Blood of Jesus, we seal our house, all those who dwell therein, (*name each one of them*), the people whom Our Lord will send to it, as well as the food and goods which He generously sends to us for our nourishment.

With the power of the Blood of Jesus, we seal all land, doors, windows, objects, walls, and floors and the air we breathe. In faith we place a circle of Thy Blood around our whole family.

With the power of the Blood of Jesus, we seal the place where we shall go during the day, the people, companies and institutions we shall have contact with today (*name each of them*).

With the power of the Blood of Jesus, we seal our material and spiritual work, the activities of the members of our family, and the vehicles, roads, air tracks, and any other form of transportation which we might use.

With Thy Precious Blood, we seal the acts, the minds, and the hearts of all the inhabitants and governors of our country, so that Thy peace and Thy Heart may reign in it.

We give Thee thanks, Lord, for Thy Blood and for Thy Life, because through them we have been saved, and we are delivered and preserved from all evil.   Amen.

Prayer to the Precious Blood Invoking the Help of Mary

O Sacred Blood, that flowed so copiously seven times for my salvation, I love Thee, I praise Thee, I adore Thee with the deepest feeling of gratitude! The purest fountain from which Thou didst flow makes Thy memory so sweet. O Precious Blood, with trumpet tones Thou speakest to me of the love of my God and Redeemer.

How I deplore my coldness and indifference towards Thee! Now, at last, I wish to return love for love, blood for Blood, if necessary. As often as my pulse beats, it shall greet Thee, Thou sweet Guest of my soul, and shall return to the arteries warmed and purified by Thy love. As long as the blood courses through my veins, it shall flow only for love of Thee; it shall circulate only for Thy interests and it shall turn cold and stand still only because I am about to love Thee in eternity. Oh, let this stream of Thy love flow through every heart and inebriate it with holy joy!

My dearest Mother Mary, I beseech Thee with confidence, obtain for me, although thy unworthy child, the blessing of God the Father, by covering me with the merits of thy Son Jesus, that I may regain my eternal birthright in

Heaven. Clothe me every evening, Sweet Lady of Mt. Carmel, but especially on the eve of my life, with the "Dyed Garments" of the Precious Blood.
Amen.

℘♦☙

<u>The Chaplet of the Holy Wounds</u>

This "Rosary" or chaplet of the Holy Wounds that was first revealed to the mystic **Sr. Marie Martha Chambon** (1841 – 1907). Our Lord revealed to her that everything that is asked of Him through the invocation of His Holy Wounds would be obtained as it is through the merit of His Precious Blood which is of infinte price through which the graces are granted.

"You will obtain everything, because it is through the merit of My Blood, which is of infinite price. With My Wounds and My Divine Heart, everything can be obtained."

The story:

Sr. Marie Martha Chambon began to report visions of Jesus in 1866 Who requested her to contemplate His Holy Wounds. Our Lord asked Sr. Chambon to unite her sufferings with His in the 'Rosary' or chaplet of the Holy Wounds as an Act of Reparation for the sins of the world. He told her that, "when you offer My Holy Wounds for sinners, you must not forget to do so for the souls in Purgatory, as there are but few who think of their relief... The Holy Wounds are the treasure of treasures for the souls in Purgatory."

This chaplet was approved for the Institute of Visitation in 1912. Sr Chambon's Mother Superior kept a chronicle of her life, which was published in 1923 and sold widely. The next year in 1924 the Vatican granted an indulgence to those who said the following prayer, based on her reported visions:

"Eternal Father I offer the wounds of Our Lord Jesus Christ, to heal the wounds of our souls."

Sr. Marie Martha Chambon's cause for beatification was introduced in 1937. The chaplet was authorized by Decree of the Congregation for the Doctrine of the Faith on March 23, 1999.

Our Lord also attached magnificent promises to this chaplet and devotions to His Holy Wounds, (listed below after the instructions).

♦

How to Pray the Chaplet

It is said on an ordinary 5 decade set of rosary beads.

Make the sign of the cross.
1. On the Crucifix / cross, pray: **"O Jesus, Divine Redeemer, be merciful to us and to the whole world. Amen."**

2. Next, on the three beads that come after the crucifix, pray on the first bead: **"Holy God, Mighty God, Immortal God, have mercy on us and on the whole world. Amen."**

3. On the second bead say: "**Grace and mercy O my Jesus, during present dangers; cover us with thy Precious Blood. Amen.**"

4. On the third bead say: "**Eternal Father, grant us mercy through the Blood of Jesus Christ, Thine only Son; grant us mercy, we beseech thee. Amen.**"

5. The five decades come next. On the single large 'Our Father' beads pray: "**Eternal Father, I offer Thee the Wounds of Our Lord Jesus Christ to heal the wounds of our souls. Amen.**"

6. On the 10 smaller 'Hail Mary' beads, pray: "**My Jesus, pardon and mercy through the merits of Thy Holy Wounds. Amen.**"

7. Conclude by saying the prayer on the large beads three times: "**Eternal Father, I offer Thee the wounds of our Lord Jesus Christ to heal the wounds of our souls. Amen.**"

♦

THE PROMISES given by Our Lord to those who practise this chaplet as revealed to Sr. Mary Martha Chambon, plus promises for devotion towards His Holy Wounds:

"I will grant all that is asked of Me by the invocation of My Holy Wounds. You must spread this devotion."

"With My Wounds and My Divine Heart you can obtain everything."

"The sinner who will say: ' Eternal Father, I offer Thee the Wounds of Our Lord Jesus Christ, etc.' will obtain conversion."

"The Holy Wounds are the treasures for the souls in Purgatory."

"The Chaplet of Mercy (i.e. the other name of the Holy Wound chaplet), is a counterpoise to My justice, it restrains My vengeance."

"At each word that you pronounce of the Chaplet of Mercy **I allow a drop of My Blood to fall upon the soul of a sinner.**"

"Each time that you offer to My Father the merits of My Divine Wounds, you win an immense fortune."

"Souls that will have contemplated and honoured My crown of thorns on earth, will be My crown of glory in Heaven!"

"I will grant all that is asked of Me through the invocation of My Holy Wounds. You will obtain everything, because it is through the merit of My Blood, which is on infinite price. With My Wounds and My Divine Heart, everything can be obtained.

"From My Wounds proceed fruits of sanctity. As gold purified in the crucible become more beautiful, so you must put your soul and those of your companions into My Sacred Wounds; there they will become perfected as gold in the furnace. You can always purify yourself in My Wounds."

"My Wounds will repair yours. My Wounds will cover all your faults. Those who honour them will have a true knowledge of Jesus Christ. In meditation on them, you will always find a new love. My Wounds will cover all your sins."

"Plunge your actions into My Wounds and they will be of value. All your actions, even the least, soaked in My Blood, will acquire by this alone an infinite merit and will please My Heart."

"In offering My Wounds for the conversion of sinners, even though the sinners are not converted, you will have the same merit before God as if they were."

"When you have some trouble, something to suffer, quickly place it in My Wounds, and the pain will be alleviated."

"This aspiration must often be repeated near the sick: "My Jesus, pardon and mercy through the merits of Thy Holy Wounds!" This prayer will solace soul and body.

"There will be no death for the soul that expires in My Holy Wounds; they give true life."

"Those who pray with humility and who meditate on My Passion, will one day participate in the glory of My Divine Wounds."

"The more you will have contemplated My painful Wounds on this earth, the higher will be your contemplation of them glorious in Heaven."

"The soul who during life has honoured the Wounds of Our Lord Jesus Christ and has offered them to the Eternal Father for the Souls in Purgatory, will be accompanied at the moment of death by the Holy Virgin and the angels; and Our

Lord on the Cross, all brilliant in glory, will receive her and crown her."

"The invocations of the Holy Wounds will obtain an incessant victory for the Church."

♦

Additional Confirmation of the Promises to the Mystic Marie-Julie Jahenny (1850 – 1941)

In the years 1939 to 1941, the 'Breton Stigmatist' Marie-Julie Jahenny received several message regarding the Chaplet of the Holy Wounds:

(November 14, 1939) Our Lady: "Don't forget to say this Rosary of the Holy Wounds that I love very much! I bring to my Divine Son the sweet words that you say in this rosary."

(June 10, 1940) (Speaking?) "It takes a lot of prayers to obtain your liberation. Add the Rosary of the Holy Wounds to your Rosary."

(Observations on 'obtain your liberation' – at the time, Marie-Julie had just added this chaplet to her dailiy prayers. World War II had started not long before this when Marie-Julie received this message, apparently, this chaplet would help bring peace, but it would take much prayer. Also, considering one of her spiritual missions was not only to pray for souls but to pray for the coming triumph of the Church, one of the promises attached to the chaplet is that the invocations of the Holy Wounds will obtain an incessant victory for the Church.)

(January 21, 1941) (Speaking to Marie-Julie? Possibly Our Lady:)

"Console yourself, the Holy Wounds are the way of salvation. Tell the little souls how much I love those who spread devotion to the Rosary of the Holy Wounds."

(Undated Text): "The devotion to the Holy Wounds will be a lightning rod for the Christians who will have kept it."

(I.e. those faithful to the devotion will be protected as a lightning rod protects from lightning strikes. Therefore, this message confirms the promise of protection and will be spared the blows of Divine Justice as Our Lord promised to Sr. Chambon this devotion "is a counterpoise to My justice, it restrains My vengeance.")

☙♦☙

Ingulgenced Prayers to the Precious Blood

ಐ♦ଓଐ♦ଓଐ♦ଓ

For the Glory of Jesus

Eternal Father, by the most Precious Blood of Jesus Christ, glorify His most Holy Name, according to the intention and the desire of His Adorable heart.

*(Indulgence 300 days, each time.
Pius X, Jan. 27, 1908)*

♦

Praised and blessed be the most Sacred Heart of Jesus and the Precious Blood of Jesus in the Most Blessed Sacrament.

(300 days indulgence, every time. Pius X, Aug 25, 1908)

♦

For the Conversion of Dying Sinners

My God, I offer Thee all the masses which are being celebrated today throughout the whole world, for sinners who are in their agony and who are to die today. May the Precious Blood of Jesus, their Redeemer, obtain mercy for them.

(300 days indulgence, once a day. Pius X, Oct. 29, 1907)

♦

O most merciful Jesus, lover of souls! I pray Thee, by the agony of Thy most Sacred Heart, and by the sorrows of Thy Immaculate Mother, cleanse in Thy own Blood the sinners of the whole world who are now in their agony and about to die. Amen. Heart of Jesus, once in agony, pity the dying.

(100 days indulgence each time. Plenary indulgence once a month if said thrice daily at three distinct intervals, plus the usual conditions.
Pius IX, Feb. 2, 1850)

♦

For Reparation and the Needs of the Church

Eternal Father, we offer Thee the Blood, Passion, and the death of Jesus Christ, the sorrows of Mary most holy, and of St. Joseph, in satisfaction for our sins, in aid of the holy souls in Purgatory, for the needs of holy Mother Church, and for the conversion of sinners.

(100 days indulgence, once a day. Pius IX, April 30, 1860)

♦

Eternal Father, I offer Thee the Precious blood of Jesus Christ, in satisfaction for my sins and for the wants of Holy Church.

(100 days indulgence, every time. Pius VII, Sept. 22, 1817)

♦

For the Souls in Purgatory

We beseech Thee, therefore, assist the souls still suffering in Purgatory, whom Thou hast redeemed with Thy Precious Blood.

(300 days indulgence, each time. Pius X, Sept. 13, 1908)

The _Anima Christi_ of St Ignatius

Soul of Christ, sanctify me.
Body of Christ, save me.
Blood of Christ, inebriate me.
Water from the side of Christ, wash me.
O good Jesus, hear me!
Within Thy Wounds hide me.
Never permit me to be separated from Thee.
From the malignant enemy defend me.
At the hour of my death call me,
And bid me come to Thee,
That with Thy saints, I may praise Thee,
For ever and ever. Amen.

(*300 days indulgence each time. 7 years after receiving Holy Communion. Pius IX, Jan. 9, 1854. Plenary if said daily for for a month under the usual conditions.*)

Quotations of St. Gaspar del Bufalo on Devotion to the Precious Blood

♦

"Blessed Gaspar del Bufalo frequently assured his contemporaries that those who foster devotion to the Precious Blood shall obtain special mercy in times of tribulation."[13]

♦

St. Gaspar: "I repeat: let us propagate widely this very important devotion; let us often meditate on those words: 'making peace through the Blood of the Cross both in the heavens and on the earth.' May Jesus be our love." (To Mr. Giovanni Francesco Palmucci, February 24, 1826, Letter 1341).

♦

St. Gaspar: "In every era the Lord has inspired certain devotions to stem the tide of iniquity. We also see that in times past the Church was attacked in this or that doctrine.

---

[13] 'Glories of the Precious Blood", Rev. Fr. Max Walz, TAN, 2010.

Today the war is being waged against religion as such and against Christ Crucified. We need, therefore, to re-emphasize the glories of the Cross and of our Crucified Redeemer, to reopen the fountains of mercy just when the devil would make us the victim of wrath. Now, more than ever, it is opportune to tell people at what price our souls were redeemed. We must let it be known how the Blood of Christ cleanses the souls and sanctifies them, particularly by means of the sacraments. We must arouse them from their insensibility by reminding them that His Blood is offered up every morning upon the altars and that instead of blasphemy and insult, we should give it adoration and praise."

♦

St. Gaspar: "Become attached in fervor to the devotion to the Divine Blood which softens every heart, and do not fail to turn frequently to the most holy Immaculate Mary under whose protection it is most helpful to remain." (*From St. Gaspar's Letter 1183 to Fr. Giovanni Chiodi, June 30, 1825*)

Illustration Credits

Page 26. "Christ with Moses and Solomon", or "The Blood of the Redeember with Moses and Solomon" (1541) by Moretto da Brescia. Frick Digital Photo Collection, public domain listing.

Page 30. "The Creation of Adam" (c. 1642), by Giovanni Benedetto Castiglione. Art Institute of Chicago, public domain.

Page 32. "Cain and Abel" (1886), etching by Odilon Redon. The Stickney Collection, Art Institute of Chicago, public domain.

Page 35. "The Mystical Grapes", early 16^{th-} century tapestry from Flanders, possibly Bruges. Cleveland Museum of Art, Creative Commons Zero, public domain.

Page 38. Illustration of the Hebrews placing the lambs blood on their doors, from the book "With the Children on Sundays, through Eye-Gate, and Ear Gate into the City of Child-Soul" (1911) by Sylvanus Stall. Photo credit: Library of Congress. No known copyright restrictions, public domain.

Page 44. "Monnik vangt het bloed van Christus", public domain image by Rijks Museum, licensed under CC0 1.0.

Page 47. "The Circumcision", etching by F.G. Aliamet, (1765), after G. Reni. Wellcome Collection, public domain.

Page 49. "Christ in Gethsemane", by Heinrich Hofmann (1886). Public Domain listing.

Page 52. "Penediment de Judes" (1874), by Simó Gómez. Public Domain listing.

Page 54. "Pilate Washing His Hands" by Mattia Preti (1663). Metropolitan Musem of Art, public domain listing.

Page 58. "The Flagellation of Christ" by Peter Paul Rubens (c. 1617.) Museum of Fine Arts Ghent (MSK), this has been made available under the Creative Commons CC0 1.0 Universal Public Domain Dedication.

Page 60. "Christ as the Man of Sorrows," engraving by W. Sharp, (1798), after G. Reni. Wellcome Collection, public domain.

Page 63. "Nailing Christ to the Cross" by Gustave Doré. Public domain image provided by:
https://creationism.org/images/DoreBibleIllus/index.htm

Page 65. "The Crucifixion of Christ; His Side is Punctured by a Soldier's Lance", engraving by B. à Bolswert after P.P. Rubens. Wellcome Collection, public domain.

Page 66. "Overwinning van het koninkrijk van Christus", Jacob Neefs, after David Herregouts, (1649). The white robed elect of the Apocalypse adore the Lamb, (above). Christ the King surrounded by the symbols of the Four Evangelists pours His Blood upon the earth, which is first gathered by Mother Church and pours fourth in seven streams representing the Sacraments. Rijks Museum, public domain image.

http://hdl.handle.net/10934/RM0001.COLLECT.157838

Page 71. "The Last Supper" by Gustave Doré, public domain image provided by:
https://creationism.org/images/DoreBibleIllus/index.htm

Page 73. "Christ with Chalice", Juan de Juanes (c.1579), public domain image, Web Gallery of Art.

Page 76. "The Adoration of the Lamb, from The Apocalypse", woodcut by Albrecht Dürer (1471-1528). Metropolitan Museum of Art, public domain.

Page 85. "Mano Poderosa" ("The All-Powerful Hand"), or "Las Cinco Personas" ("The Five Persons"), Mexico, 19th century. Oil on metal (possibly tin-plated iron). Brooklyn Museum. No known copyright restriction.

Page 92. "Christ Crowned with Thorns" by Aelbrecht Bouts, (C. 1449, 1455.) Musée des beaux-arts de Lyon, public domain listing, no known copyright restrictions.

Page 103. "The crucified Christ bleeds into cups held by attending angels", woodcut. Wellcome Collection, public domain.

Page 107. "The Grieving Virgin, with a Chalice of the Precious Blood, the Nails, and the Lance". Anonymous, Flemish School, active 17th century. Public domain photo from the Frick Digital Collection.

Page 114. "Veneration of the Holy Wounds", illustration in the Printed Book of Hours (Use of Rome)- (fol. 53r, Pieta – 2009.276.53.a), by Guillaume Le Rouge. Image: Cleveland Museum of Art, Creative Commons Zero, Public Domain Dedication.

Page 122. "An Angel Holding a Chalice", by Giambattista Pittoni, (1687-1767). Public Domain photo from the Frick Digital Collection.

Page 137. "Ecce Homo", photo of a statue. No information given with image, no known copyright restrictions for photo in author's possession.

Page 142. "The Holy Face" *(La sainte face)*, 1886-1894 by James Tissot. Brooklyn Museum, no known copyright restrictions.

If you liked this book you will also like these by Fr. Marin de Boylesve

Little Month of Saint Joseph

ISBN: 978-989-96844-8-5

The Month of Saint Michael

ISBN: 978-989-96844-92

The Sacred Heart of Jesus

ISBN: 978-989-33-2807-1

A Thought for Each Day of the Year

ISBN: 978-989-33-1995-6

www.ingramcontent.com/pod-product-compliance
Lightning Source LLC
La Vergne TN
LVHW091300080426
835510LV00007B/338